PRAISE FOR *FIRST PLACE*

First Place is the healthiest way to lose weight *and* keep a spiritual atmosphere in your life. Prayer *does* change things in body, mind and spirit!

MARGE CALDWELL
AUTHOR, SPEAKER, MARRIAGE COUNSELOR

First Place has given me the opportunity to present Jesus as the only One who can make a lasting difference in a person's life—spiritually, mentally, emotionally and physically.

JIM CLAYTON
PASTOR
DIXIE LEE BAPTIST CHURCH
LENOIR CITY, TENNESSEE

First Place is inspiring, motivational, educational and challenging; and that is just the first chapter. Read on.

RICHARD COUEY
PROFESSOR OF HEALTH SCIENCES
BAYLOR UNIVERSITY
WACO, TEXAS

The First Place program is a recognized resource for individuals and churches around the country. Now, *First Place* puts the principles of this effective program within the reach of multitudes.

JIM FLORENCE, DR.P.H., CHES
ASSISTANT PROFESSOR
DEPARTMENT OF PUBLIC HEALTH
EAST TENNESSEE STATE UNIVERSITY
JOHNSON CITY, TENNESSEE

First Place is the finest program available for individuals concerned about being totally healthy. First Place is health for the soul, mind, body and spirit—it's the real thing!

BILL HESTON
VICE PRESIDENT FOR UNIVERSITY ADVANCEMENT
HOWARD PAYNE UNIVERSITY

From the moment I met Carole Lewis, she had a passion to help people achieve balance in their physical and spiritual lives. First Place has grown into an international program that encourages men and women to be Christian examples to a searching world.

FLORENCE LITTAUER
AUTHOR, *SILVER BOXES; PERSONALITY PLUS; TAKING CHARGE OF YOUR LIFE*
FOUNDER, CLASS SPEAKERS

I joyfully testify to the biblical integrity of the First Place program and the spiritual authenticity of those in leadership. God's way has worked for Carole, it has worked for me, and it will work for you!

BETH MOORE
AUTHOR, *BREAKING FREE; PRAYING GOD'S WORD*

A minister is often so busy that the "temple of the Holy Spirit" is neglected. For me First Place has proven to be a strategic plan for balancing the demands on body, mind, soul and spirit.

DAVID SELF
ASSOCIATE PASTOR
HOUSTON FIRST BAPTIST CHURCH
HOUSTON, TEXAS

First Place is a true wellness program, balancing proven principles of lifestyle change with Bible study, prayer, Scripture memory, the support of fellow believers and a healthy eating and physical activity plan. I wholeheartedly recommend this book and the First Place program.

JODY WILKINSON, M.D., M.S.
PHYSICIAN AND EXERCISE PSYCHOLOGIST
COOPER INSTITUTE
DALLAS, TEXAS

I learned more about nutrition and healthy eating in my first session of First Place than I did in my culinary classes. But after only a couple of weeks, the diet portion (or the Live-It, as we call it) became secondary to the spiritual food I was being fed.

SCOTT WILSON, C.E.C., A.A.C.
CHEF/OWNER, HEALTHY HOME COOKING!

FIRST PLACE

CAROLE LEWIS
WITH W. TERRY WHALIN

Regal

A Division of Gospel Light
Ventura, California, U.S.A.

Published by Regal Books
A Division of Gospel Light
Ventura, California, U.S.A.
Printed in the U.S.A.

Regal Books is a ministry of Gospel Light, an evangelical Christian publisher dedicated to serving the local church. We believe God's vision for Gospel Light is to provide church leaders with biblical, user-friendly materials that will help them evangelize, disciple and minister to children, youth and families.

It is our prayer that this Regal book will help you discover biblical truth for your own life and help you meet the needs of others. May God richly bless you.

For a free catalog of resources from Regal Books/Gospel Light, please call your Christian supplier or contact us at 1-800-4-GOSPEL or www.regalbooks.com.

All Scripture quotations, unless otherwise indicated, are taken from the *Holy Bible, New International Version*®. Copyright © 1973, 1978, 1984 by International Bible Society. Used by permission of Zondervan Publishing House. All rights reserved.

Other versions used are:
KJV—King James Version. Authorized King James Version.
NLT—Scripture quotations marked (*NLT*) are taken from the *Holy Bible*, New Living Translation, copyright © 1996. Used by permission of Tyndale House Publishers, Inc., Wheaton, IL 60189. All rights reserved.
TLB—Scripture quotations marked (*TLB*) are taken from *The Living Bible*, copyright © 1971. Used by permission of Tyndale House Publishers, Inc., Wheaton, IL 60189. All rights reserved.

Caution
The information contained in this book is intended to be solely informational and educational. It is assumed that the First Place participant will consult a medical or health professional before beginning this or any other weight-loss or physical fitness program.

Cover Design by Barbara LeVan Fisher
Interior Design by Rob Williams
Original edition edited by Janis Whipple
Revised edition edited by Rose Decaen

Library of Congress Cataloging-in-Publication Data

Lewis, Carole, 1942-
    First place/Carole Lewis with W. Terry Whalin. – Rev. ed.
        p. cm.
    Includes bibliographical references.
    ISBN 0-8307-2863-5
        1. Weight loss—Religious aspects—Christianity. 2. Health—Religious aspects—Christianity. I.
Whalin, Terry. II. Title.

RM222.2 .L446 2001
613.2'5—dc21   2001019707

1 2 3 4 5 6 7 8 9 10 11 12 13 14 15 / 09 08 07 06 05 04 03 02 01

Rights for publishing this book in other languages are contracted by Gospel Literature International (GLINT). GLINT also provides technical help for the adaptation, translation and publishing of Bible study resources and books in scores of languages worldwide. For further information, write to GLINT, P.O. Box 4060, Ontario, CA 91761-1003, U.S.A. You may also send e-mail to Glintint@aol.com, or visit the GLINT website at www.glint.org.

CONTENTS

⁎

March 2001 marks the 20th Anniversary of the First Place program, and as I reminisce about the early days of First Place, I know I must give special thanks to:

Dottie Brewer, the founder of the program;

Marilyn Stelly, who so faithfully typed all of the first manuscripts;

Buddy Griffin, who believed so strongly in the program that he went to bat to make it become a reality;

Kelly Roberts, who wrote the very first Bible study;

Barbara Grogan, Lois McCall, Dr. William Heston, Sally Johnson, Susan Crawford, Bobby Boyles and **Beth Moore,** each of whom authored the Bible studies that followed; and

Our First Place staff in Houston, whose prayers and support are evidence of the wonderful blessings that come about in the workplace when Christ is given first place.

Lastly, all of us at First Place want to take this opportunity to say thank you to all of you who have contributed to the growth of the First Place program. It would take pages and pages to list each and every person who has worked untold hours for God's glory. I am reminded of the song "Thank You" by Ray Boltz that says, "Thank you for giving to the Lord. I am a life that was changed." May the next 20 years bear as much Kingdom fruit as the last 20!

What direction have you chosen for your life? Take a look beyond this day or this hour and look at the overall picture of your health—emotionally, physically, spiritually and mentally. How do you measure up to your own expectations? More importantly, how do you evaluate yourself compared to God's standard? These complex questions have no simple answers.

Many years ago as a young married woman with three small children, I heard Dr. Ralph Neighbor, a missionary, discussing telling others about Jesus Christ. He said that witnessing is nothing but one hungry beggar telling another where to find the bread. Throughout the years, those words have been driven into my mind and heart, yet their meaning goes beyond how I share my faith with other people. For me, the Christian life symbolizes one hungry beggar telling another where to find the Bread—the Lord Jesus Christ. Jesus Himself said in John 6:35, "I am the bread of life. He who comes to me will never go hungry, and he who believes in me will never be thirsty." True satisfaction in life is only discovered as we hunger and thirst after Jesus Christ.

You will find that First Place is about a process where we fellow pilgrims are on a journey, learning more every day about how to follow Jesus. Do we listen as He tells us not worry because He is guiding us? He tells us in Matthew 6:28-30 that God will take care of us, He will meet all of our needs. Yet we must seek Him above all of these needs: "Seek first his kingdom and his righteousness, and all these things will be given to you as well" (Matt. 6:33). Yet we in our impatience want all these "things" without seeking His kingdom before all else.

You have selected this book for a reason. The "thing" you want may be to lose a specific amount of weight. Or perhaps your goal is to lose weight to raise your self-esteem—or fit into that swimsuit. Yet the critical question this book will address again and again is whether you are willing to go through the process of spiritual growth necessary to have these "things" added to your life.

The process involves turning to God every day, giving Him the highest priority—first place—in every area of your life. This book offers specific guidance about how to move along the path of seeking God's kingdom in your life.

Dear friend, as your read about the program we call First Place, I pray that it reveals more than simply another diet. Instead, I pray that you will discover your Friend and mine, Jesus Christ. He is the Bread of Life. May God bless your search for the One who can change your life.

Carole Lewis
First Place National Director

✳

A CHALLENGE
FOR AMERICA

America is full of fabulous grocery stores. The shelves are loaded with such variety that our minds spin when even trying to determine which type of cereal to buy. We have the largest selection of fresh vegetables, fruits and meats in the world. Shelves are filled with fresh baked breads, pies, cakes and cookies prepared in the store or brought in from local bakeries. You have the choice of many varieties and brands of milk, cheese and yogurt. Canned goods and packaged items are abundant, and the aisles of frozen foods seem endless.

Besides our grocery stores, we have restaurants on every corner. Even the smallest of towns has a couple of fast-food restaurants and a local cafe. The variety of restaurants is endless. Americans can choose foods from anywhere in the world. We can take out or eat inside. Most of us have easy access to every kind of food imaginable.

America also has the finest medical facilities in the world. There are medical centers in every major city, with doctors who specialize in every illness known to man. Yet despite all these potential advantages, we still have the reputation of being the unhealthiest developed nation in the world. Health professionals tell us our health problems are due to our poor eating habits and our sedentary lifestyles.

John Graham, director of Harvard's Center for Risk Analysis in Boston, says that "by changing personal behavior, people could reduce their risk of dying early by 70 percent to 80 percent." Professor Graham also says, "The number one and number three killers in America are heart disease and stroke, which often are caused by a fatty diet, failure to exercise, high cholesterol and high blood pressure. The number two and number four killers are cancer and lung disease, which may be brought on by the choices we make."[1]

Most Americans who are aware of their own obesity generally try dieting at one point or another. Many try losing the weight by going on crash diets found in their favorite magazines or in books from their local bookstores. Others may try liquid diet plans where they deprive themselves of solid food and, many times, the necessary nutrients for their bodies. However, studies of weight loss show that these types of crash diets in general don't work. As soon as a person ends a particular diet, the weight returns. Studies show that 95 percent of people who lose weight gain it back within two years.

A NATIONAL FIXATION ON WEIGHT LOSS

Every year, Americans spend $33 billion on weight-reduction programs and products, but the goods don't seem to do much good! The number of overweight Americans increased from 25 percent in 1980 to 33 percent in 1991. According to the National Health and Nutrition Examination Survey, 11 percent of children and adolescents are overweight, up from about 5 percent in the 1970s. At any given time, 33 to 40 percent of women are trying to lose weight, and 20 to 24 percent of men are dieting.[2]

The weight-loss craze is the second most popular recreational means of spending money, topped only by fitness. During the months of January and September, full-page newspaper ads lure us into one program or another to lose weight. Weight-loss professionals understand that most Americans think about weight loss more during these two times of the year than any other time. New Year's resolutions spark the interest in January; people see this month as a great time to lose any weight gained since Halloween. September is the second choice to lose weight because we want to be ready to stuff ourselves during the Thanksgiving and Christmas seasons.

As a society, we are now consumed with thoughts about weight and exercise. Many of us are on a search for a quick fix. At the same time, we are unwilling to consider permanent changes in our lifestyles. Some programs tell us to eat foods high in protein and low in carbohydrates to lose weight. Others advise the exact opposite. There are programs that tell us to eliminate certain food groups like milk and meat from our diet, while others say that the key to weight loss is to juice our fruits and vegetables and eat everything raw. Another program teaches that God created every food, and if we pray and study our Bible but still want Ding-Dongs or Twinkies, that's OK; we just need to stop eating when we're full. Other programs sell us our food; our only task in order to lose weight is to heat and eat those foods. The problem with this method is that we still have to learn to prepare nutritious food after we have lost the weight.

Some men and women have taken drastic measures to lose weight—such as having a physician staple their stomachs. Then they can only consume a couple of tablespoons of food at one time. However, even with such a severe measure, many people still find ways to eat too much and remain overweight. Another alarming weight-loss method is the use of drugs to curb the appetite. In the 1960s and 1970s, diet pills were prescribed to those wanting to lose weight; these pills were amphetamines. Amphetamines suppress appetite; however, they made those who took them wired and addicted. Other drugs replaced amphetamines. These new drugs increased brain chemicals that affected moods and suppressed the appetite.

A SAFE WEIGHT-LOSS PROGRAM

Almost every day in the newspaper and news magazines, so-called authorities bombard us with health information, telling us that if we don't do it their way, then we are doomed to failure or a lifetime of poor health. Since pesticides are killing us, we are cautioned to buy only organic meats and produce. Other news articles proclaim that our foods have no vitamins left, so we must megadose on vitamin and mineral supplements. We are left unsure about what is factual and what is not.

This plethora of weight-loss programs and information stirs mass confusion about how to take weight off and lose it permanently. We then look in the mirror and see we are still fat despite losing hundreds of pounds in our lifetime.

What can be done?

To help us sort through the confusion surrounding weight loss, we turned to Dr. Dick Couey, a professor of health sciences at Baylor University and a physiologist who has studied nutrition and how it relates to the biochemistry of the cell. On a regular basis, Dr. Couey gives his opinion about the safety or effectiveness of certain diets. His criteria for a good diet includes the following:

1. The diet must contain the 45 known nutrients in their proper amounts. It must contain enough carbohydrate, fat and protein (especially nitrogen); 9 amino acids; 13 vitamins; 19 minerals; and sufficient amounts of water.
2. The diet should contain at least 1,200 calories per day. Caloric consumption below 1,200 could possibly cause damage to your body and permanently lower its basal metabolism.
3. The diet should emphasize behavior modification techniques to overcome poor eating habits or problem eating. It should also stress ways to make lifestyle changes in order to facilitate weight maintenance and thwart further weight gain.
4. The diet should not only stress good eating practices but also emphasize regular physical activity, stress reduction and other healthy changes in lifestyle. In addition, Dr. Couey recommends a Christian emphasis to help motivate participants to properly care for their bodies.

"Be very careful about choosing other nutritional programs," concludes Dr. Couey. "Many of these programs are designed to help you lose weight; however, they may lack the proper amounts of nutrients which can damage the health of the cells."

Dr. Couey includes a caution about selecting a diet program:

Fad diets usually don't work because they are not designed for permanent weight loss. Habits are not changed, and the food selection is so limited that the person cannot follow the diet for more than two or three weeks. Although dieters assume they have lost fat, they have actually lost mostly muscle and other lean tissue mass. In a matter of weeks, most of the lost weight is back. The dieter appears to have failed, when actually the diet failed. The whole scenario can add more blame and guilt to the psyche of the dieter, which is very unfortunate.

In his final bit of advice, Dr. Couey extends hope, saying, "If someone needs help losing weight, First Place is the answer. My wish for you is expressed beautifully in 3 John 2 which says, 'I pray that you may enjoy good health and that all may go well with you, even as your soul is getting along well.'"[3]

HOPE AHEAD

When it comes to weight loss, you may wonder if anyone can find hope. Yes, I believe you can. In the chapters that follow, I will detail a program called First Place. After an initial overview of the program along with my personal experience and that of several others, we will look at motivation and the various obstacles to weight loss. Next we will consider what the Bible has to do with a weight-loss program and why it is critical to have a spiritual foundation to a weight-loss program. First Place is more than weight loss—it's a lifestyle change that encourages every participant to find balance in his or her own life. Balance is the topic for a separate chapter. The third and final section of the book examines the First Place program in detail. This section includes some ready-to-use tools and nine distinct commitments that are a part of the program. I'll also detail additional possibilities beyond the basic program, such as Fitness Weeks, conferences and training programs. In the final pages of this book, we will look beyond weight-loss specifics—I want to give you a great dosage of hope and a plan for lifestyle changes that show you the reality of Jesus in everyday life.

While the text portion of this book finishes in an uplifting fashion, it's not the final page of the book. Don't ignore the appendices at the back of the book. They are loaded with helpful information such the Live-It food exchange program and a variety of resources to help you begin a First Place group.

Throughout my years with First Place, I've met numerous people who have each lost more than 100 pounds using this program. Initially I am amazed at the transformation in a single individual; such a weight loss seems impossible. Then I remember that these people didn't lose their weight overnight; they did it over a period of months or years. What's more, they are keeping that weight off—permanently. You may be scared to take such a journey or even to entertain the possibility of losing weight permanently. If so, consider the Chinese proverb, "The journey of a thousand miles begins with a single step."

Turn the page and let's take the first step to learn about the First Place program.

✳

CHAPTER ONE

PUTTING GOD IN FIRST PLACE

At age four, Karen Arnett spent a few months with her grandparents. When her parents arrived to take her home, they hardly recognized Karen because she had gained so much weight. As she says, "My grandmother fed me very well." Despite Karen's active childhood, she remained overweight.

Today when Karen considers the main reason she overate, she says it was from boredom. "If I was having a bad day with the kids or a financial problem or a fight with my husband, I ate." Food was Karen's reward and comfort. Her weight steadily increased to 416 pounds. At her home in Evans, Georgia, Karen started a low-fat diet plan in December 1994 and lost 68 pounds. While the low-fat plan was helping, she knew it wasn't the total answer to her health needs. Karen says, "I wasn't submitting my life to God completely. I still overate and didn't exercise."

In May 1995, Karen started the First Place program and now sees how God has blessed every area of her life. Her dress size has gone from a 56 to a 10/12 and Karen has lost 83½ inches and a total of 261 pounds. Since January 1997, Karen has maintained her weight at 155 pounds. A shy person by nature, at one time Karen found it difficult to say anything and usually stood in the back of a room. "It wasn't until I found First Place that I realized only God could truly help me. Only by committing all of my life to Him and disciplining myself could I overcome my eating problems," Karen says. Through the program her life has changed drastically, and Karen sees this change as evidence of God's power. "When I was overweight, I was not a testimony to God and His power in my life. Now God has used the weakest area of my life to exhibit His power."

WHAT IS FIRST PLACE?

Since the First Place program began in 1981, it has spread to all 50 states and over 12,000 churches from various denominations. First Place is also active in at least 13 foreign countries. Yet most of you have probably never heard of First Place. It has no huge advertising budget, and no marketing efforts have been made to get the word out about the program. Those of us involved in First Place have given the program over to God for His glory, and I often say God is our publicist. Most of the growth has come from word-of-mouth customers and the enthusiasm of people who have been through the program.

It all began during the late 1970s. A group of Christians in the First Baptist Church in Houston, Texas, had one question: Since God has saved us from our sins and given us an abundant life, why can't we, as Christians, use that same power in the area of weight control? These people recognized that the spiritual life involved discipline. It takes discipline to pray and follow God every day. By the same token, it takes discipline to control our food consumption. The key desire of these Christians was to create a Christ-centered weight-control program. With this firm goal in mind, they faced it—fully unaware of the immensity of the assignment.

The program would focus totally on Christ and include Bible study, small-group support, a proven commonsense nutrition plan, a method of record keeping and many other elements. These early leaders knew that the key was to keep Christ first in every aspect of the program. And weight loss was not their only focus; they also aimed to grow in every area of life: spiritual, mental, emotional and physical. A key concept of the program was—and is—balance.

The logo for First Place illustrates the balance of the program. Each of the four aspects of life is given equal importance. Through Christ, we can achieve balance in all four areas of life if we depend on Him daily to satisfy our hunger. Jesus also taught that God's Word is central to achieving this by saying in Matthew 4:4, "It is written: 'Man does not live on bread alone, but on every word that comes from the mouth of God.'" Through studying God's Word, we find that it provides guidelines for our physical well-being, directs us spiritually and equips us mentally to manage our busy lives. When we are students of His Word, God also provides emotional stability by giving us understanding of His precepts and the ability through the Holy Spirit to apply them in crisis and everyday situations.

If you are facing physical hunger, as you pray to God, He can provide for your daily physical needs. If you are facing spiritual, emotional or mental hunger, the Bible is also the answer to your needs.

WHAT ARE THE NINE COMMITMENTS?

The First Place program includes a series of nine commitments which will be explained in detail in chapters 6 and 7. In brief, these commitments include:

1. *Attendance*. A key part of this program is commitment to a small group of people for a 13-week session. This group will be critical as you keep the other eight commitments; therefore, it is essential that you attend every meeting and stay for the entire session. (If you cannot locate a group or begin a group in your area, you will need to find two or three other friends to help you with accountability to the program.)

2. *Encouragement.* You make a commitment to reach out to another class member in your group every week. The contact gives you a chance to share with others in your group when you are tempted and to ask them for prayer. Your phone call, card or e-mail may be an encouragement for other class members when they are tempted and in need of support. Sometimes you may feel great yourself and not feel the need to contact anyone, but another member may be in need. The Holy Spirit may prompt you to reach out to this person and encourage him or her. Many times the person you contact may be feeling discouraged and even be in the process of overeating, but your phone call, card or e-mail of encouragement may be the one thing he or she needs to face temptation.

3. *Prayer.* As you pray every day at the same time, it will help you keep Christ in first place in your life. God is concerned about your eating habits and food consumption. Prayer will be critical preparation to overcoming the temptation to eat the wrong food, and prayer will see you through every day. As you communicate with God, you will build a closer relationship with your heavenly Father. Prayer is also an important part of the First Place meetings, where group members pray for each other's needs every week.

4. *Bible reading.* The Bible says in John 8:32, "You will know the truth, and the truth will set you free." So often we avoid the truth from God's Word, yet this commitment is essential for spiritual growth. Regular reading from the Bible provides the foundation for a spiritual fitness plan. The First Place Scripture reading plan includes a daily Bible reading from the Old and New Testaments. Each day's reading can be thoughtfully read in 15 to 30 minutes.

5. *Scripture memory verse.* First Place involves memorizing a Bible verse each week and repeating it daily. The memory verse connects to the Bible lesson and provides daily strength and encouragement. God's Word in your heart will strengthen your daily life and spiritual relationship.

6. *Bible study*. This 10-week study is not meant to be intense. Every day you should read, meditate on and answer a small portion of that week's Bible study. Regular Bible study will build your spiritual fitness as you build your physical fitness.

7. *Live-It plan*. The word "diet" sounds too morbid for a Christian program. When Christ is in first place, the Christian life is meant to be lived abundantly. In First Place we use the term "live-it" instead of "diet" (die-it). Through this commitment, you learn balanced eating habits. In Appendix A, I explain the size of a portion which we call an exchange. The food exchange list is similar to one recommended by the American Diabetic Association; and the foods are divided into six different groups: milk, vegetable, fruit, bread, meat and fat. In First Place, we ask you to cut down your sugar consumption—which includes honey—until you reach your goal weight. Also, we encourage you to reduce your intake of salt and caffeine. Following these food exchanges will be critical to your weight loss.

8. *Commitment Record*. The Commitment Record (CR) increases your awareness of what you eat each day. At first, the CR may seem time-consuming, but actually it should only take a few minutes each day. The CR builds accountability into the overall First Place program and helps you more easily control your calorie intake. The daily record also reveals, in a concrete fashion, your patterns of eating. If you are attending a group, the CR is turned in each week to your small-group leader, who reads your CR and evaluates your week of eating. Your leader then helps you with any problem you might be having.

9. *Exercise*. This commitment is based on 1 Corinthians 3:16, which says, "Don't you know that you yourselves are God's temple and that God's Spirit lives in you?" What is the condition of God's house—your body? Are you ashamed of its size? If your body needs fixing, now is the time to do it. You cannot expect to maintain any degree of physical fitness without some sort of exercise program. Aerobic exercise may mean

joining an organized aerobic exercise class. Or you could walk briskly, jog or bicycle several miles. Swimming is also an excellent aerobic exercise, especially if you have joint problems. To get fit, you will need to exercise four or five times a week; to maintain fitness, you will need to exercise three times a week. Flexibility and strength training are every bit as important as aerobic exercise and should be added to your personal exercise program for total fitness.

You may be saying to yourself, *Nine different commitments! Wow! How will I ever manage to keep all nine?* They may look overwhelming, but these key ingredients are necessary, if you desire to put Christ in first place in your life. Most of us will not be able to keep all nine commitments every day, but do strive to adhere to the commitments as much as you can, relying on the strength God provides. These commitments are our goal and when we reach this goal, it will bring balance into our lives. I heard it said once like this: "God loves us just the way we are, but too much to let us stay that way"—an encouraging thought, isn't it?

When you do commit to God, expect the unexpected. Romans 8:29 says that God wants us to conform to the image of Jesus Christ. God wants to infiltrate every area of our lives, and we believe that First Place covers every major area of life. As change occurs, it can be quite dramatic. Frequently I meet men and women who say they initially joined First Place to lose weight, yet after they reached their goal weight, these same people say the most significant changes in their lives were actually spiritual ones. As we put Jesus Christ in first place, many unexpected blessings will flow into our lives. With God's help we can grow every day to be more like Jesus Christ.

WHY AM I IN FIRST PLACE?

As the director of the First Place program since 1987, the passion of my life is to follow Jesus Christ every day. However, this passion wasn't there when I initially learned about First Place.

In 1980 I attended a baby shower and I saw my friend Kay for the first time in several years. Although we had grown up together and shared many experiences, I now saw that something had changed. I said, "Kay, how could you do this to me?"

She looked a bit puzzled and said, "Do what?"

I answered, "How could you lose weight and not tell me?"

Kay smiled and said, "Carole, have you forgotten that we are going to be 40 next year? Do you want to be fat and 40?"

Her honesty shocked me. I had never combined the words "fat" and "forty." For many years I had tried repeatedly to lose 40 pounds. When I was 13 years old, I started dieting and from then on I tried almost every available weight-loss plan. Over the years I seemed to gain and lose the same 20 pounds. I could not keep those 20 pounds from returning on any plan I tried. My conversation with Kay reminded me of this vicious cycle and I thought, *Here I am again, with the same 20 pounds, and yes, I'm going to be 40 next year.*

In Jeremiah 29:11 God said, "I know the plans I have for you . . . plans to prosper you and not to harm you, plans to give you hope and a future." Little did I know when I read in our church paper about a new weight-loss program called First Place that it would be there that God would begin His plans for my change. As I attended the First Place orientation, I thought to myself, *I am not all that sure that God cares much about my losing weight.* I thought He must be interested in much bigger things. However, I reminded myself of what Kay had said about being fat and 40, and I registered for that first session.

I believe God did want me to lose those 20 pounds, but He also saw my inner rebellion. He would use First Place and the small-group accountability there to help me surrender much more to Him. As I began the program, I didn't see the need to follow the food plan because I had lost weight with a low-carbohydrate diet previously. I thought to myself, *Why try something different?* I did not eat any bread or fruit, and I ate only four or five different kinds of vegetables with all the meat and fat I wanted, as long as it added up to 1,200 calories. Each week, my leader would evaluate my Commitment Record with dismay and write on it, "Carole, what are you doing?" In hindsight, I now see that not following the food plan was another sign of my unwillingness to surrender to God's control.

I eventually ended up losing 20 pounds because I stayed within the 1,200 calories a day, despite my leader's encouragement to change my food habits. Although I was not eating by the program's Live-It food plan, I still loved the Bible study and fellowship and was content to stay with it. My success with losing the weight caught the attention of Dottie Brewer, one of the founders of the program. My First Place leader at that time then told Dottie that I had leadership potential. That is when I was asked to become a First Place leader myself. Petrified that I now had to teach a food plan that I did not know or follow, I began frantically to learn all I could to teach it. I did finally learn it and began teaching a Tuesday women's class in September 1981.

For three years, I led a class in my own strength. However, things began to change in my life. I was about to undergo a tremendous amount of turmoil. Because the Houston economy bottomed out during those years, our family was undergoing financial difficulties. My husband worked hard to save his business, but he finally had to let go of it in 1984. In the process, we lost everything except our home. As an independent person, I had not had to depend on anyone. Suddenly I did not have a car, so I had to depend on other people for my transportation.

I went to work in the education department at my church, First Baptist Houston, in August 1984. Our family was at a low point in our lives. In mid-December of that year, God showed me that all our family had been going through was a means to draw me to Him—to give up my rebellious ways and let Him become Lord of everything about me.

Many years earlier, I had given my life to Jesus Christ and I called Him Lord, but in reality, I had no idea how to let God be the Lord of my life. How could I give my life to God when I had been running it on my own for so many years? God was to answer my question a couple of weeks later when our pastor, Dr. John Bisagno, preached a sermon on the will. He said, "You might be here this morning and you know God wants to change your will. God will not come in and work on your will without your permission. If you will just pray this prayer this morning: 'Lord, I'm not willing, but I'm willing to be made willing,' then God will have permission to work on your will."

That Sunday morning, with the greatest sincerity I could muster, I prayed, "Lord, that's where I am today. I'm scared to death of what You might do with my life if I give You control of every part. But it can't be any worse than the way it is right now. My family is in a terrible mess and I feel like I'm such a mess spiritually and emotionally. So I give You permission to work on my will." Then I tacked a PS onto my prayer: "And please, God, don't let it hurt too much." In my mind, if someone was at the center of God's will, it had to be painful. For me the most painful choice would be if God sent me to Africa or China, since I certainly didn't want to go there. While I had no idea where God would take my simple prayer, I had found the key to change. I was willing to be willing. Many choices came later, but this choice was the starting place.

In October 1984, I began a walking program; then three months later I started jogging. I was a jogger for many years until I developed some knee problems and now I am walking again. Over the years, I have added flexibility and strength training to my workout routine. This type of consistency was impossible—even in my dreams—when I started First Place. Throughout my entire life, I had never been consistent at anything! Everything I attempted was a start-and-stop proposition. God wanted to see consistency in many different areas where I failed to follow through. I love the patience and long-suffering of our heavenly Father. Bit by bit, God gets the job done in our lives as we allow Him to work. Besides this area of exercise, God was teaching me to trust Him completely. It was a great lesson in my life about the importance of relationships.

A year before my personal crisis, the First Place program began to move beyond First Baptist Houston. Some of the people who had completed the First Place program in our church had moved to other churches. They asked, "How can we do First Place in our new church? This program is too wonderful to give up."

At the time, First Place didn't have a full-time staff person and Dottie Brewer, the founder of the program, volunteered 20 to 30 hours a week. She was a person who jumped into a situation and got the job done. In the early years, First Baptist Houston had to loan us money to get started. Dottie made sure this money was returned and First Place was able to stand on its own.

In 1984, she presented the program to a Dallas publisher and proposed selling the program to them. They wanted to make it available to the public through Christian bookstores. However, on the way back to Houston, Dottie prayed and felt God wanted to keep the program at First Baptist Houston. Dottie became concerned that people would use the book without one key ingredient, the small-group accountability. (Though it is not necessary to be in a First Place small group for the rest of the program to work effectively, the importance of accountability is crucial for support. Therefore, if a small group is not available in your area, the First Place program recommends you meet with two or three friends to keep accountable.) Dottie felt if individuals bought a book about First Place in a bookstore, they would try the program without even seeking the support of a group. Instead, she felt it would be better if the program grew at a slower pace, so she and the others could train leaders to use it properly. As people asked about First Place, we helped them start a program and by July 1987, the program had spread to about 50 churches.

The secretary who handled the clerical duties related to First Place planned to take a maternity leave. The church's minister of activities approached me about taking over the First Place program. He had confidence in my love for the program and my ability to take over as the director of First Place. My initial months as the director of First Place were extremely hectic. I took orders for materials, opened the new accounts, shipped the materials and then followed through with billing. Over time, the church hired more staff to help me with the ordering and customer service. We created numerous resources and made them available to those who were interested in First Place.

When I stepped into the position of director, I had no idea of the heartbreak that lay ahead. In the fall of 1987, Dottie became ill and despite numerous tests, the doctors couldn't diagnosis her illness. In July 1988, they diagnosed colon cancer—she would not have many months to live. Along with Kay Smith, who later became my associate, I spent many hours at Dottie's bedside. Whenever Dottie wanted us to be near her, we were there. By being a part of her life, I learned about the consistency of Dottie's prayer life and the depth of her spirituality. God also worked in my heart during this time of pain and grief.

Dottie had been an exercise walker for 15 years and she could walk a 15-minute mile. In fact, when Dottie and I began exercising together, I had to jog beside her because of her fast walking pace. Now in the hospital, Dottie had a strong heart, but her body was frail and weak. However, Dottie never lost her sense of humor. About three weeks before her death, propped up on some pillows and reflecting on how it all began, Dottie told me, "Carole, of all people, I would never have chosen you as the director of First Place." We had a good laugh about God's unusual sense of humor. I am sure she marveled at how God uses those who surrender late in life, or anytime, for His glory. She went home to be with the Lord on March 22, 1989, only eight months after she had been diagnosed with cancer. In many ways, First Place continues as a legacy to Dottie Brewer.

In my years as the director of First Place, the program has exploded in growth and many products to support our program have been created. My starting point was certainly not very glorious, yet God was present in every decision. From the moment we accept Jesus as our personal Savior, God promises to invade our lives and never leave us. As we yield our lives into God's capable hands, He molds us into the people that we need to be. My daily passion with the First Place program has been to follow God's leading and will for my life. I'm willing to be willing.

What about your will? Are you willing to be willing? You've picked up this book and have read this far because you have a need in your life. God wants to fill that void in your total life picture—physically, emotionally, mentally and spiritually.

In the next chapter we want to examine motivations. What is the proper motivation for lifestyle choices and habits? What are improper motivations and how do we overcome them? Let's turn the page and take another step along our journey to wholeness in God's eyes.

❋

CHAPTER TWO

DIG DOWN DEEP— WHAT'S YOUR MOTIVATION?

At the orientation session for First Place, Bill Patterson was worried. He felt that his life was a spiritual mess. As a Christian for almost nine years, Bill had never taken a single problem to the Lord. "While I was confident that I was a Christian, there was a huge spiritual gulf in my life," Bill says. "I never read the Bible and only prayed when I was forced to do so. We regularly attended church, but I had no active faith."

Weight loss was the major reason Bill joined a First Place group. "I didn't know how to eat, and when it came to convenience food, I was worse than everyone else, eating bags of chips and fried food," he says. "Food was essential for any celebration—a birthday, Christmas or just getting together with friends." Bill had been heavy most of his life, but he wasn't sure exactly how heavy until he joined a First Place group.

"It had been almost 10 years since I had stepped on a scale," Bill admitted. "I even skipped regular physical exams because I knew the nurse would want to weigh me. I knew my weight would be around 300, but I had no idea it would be 310 pounds the first night." Like many people, Bill wanted to deny there was a problem with his weight. One means of accomplishing that denial is to avoid stepping on a scale.

Bill started the program in June 1996 along with his wife, Angie. Both of them have lost weight and are maintaining their weight-loss goals. Bill went from 310 pounds to 185 pounds in a little over 10 months' time. An ExxonMobil businessman, Bill travels frequently. Because he now looks so different from his driver's license picture, he gets a lot of questions at the airline ticket counters. "What happened to you?"

"I've had the opportunity to tell thousands of people about what Christ has done in my life," Bill says. "Before First Place I was introverted and lacked self-confidence, both in my work and in my witness for Christ. Now, after losing my weight, I've shared my testimony on Christian radio and at churches and conferences around the country. I have also shared what God has done in my life in the business world, motivating hundreds of my peers to improve their health and in many cases improve their walk with the Lord."

WRONG REASONS FOR MAKING A LIFESTYLE CHANGE

Throughout this book, I describe a holistic program of lifestyle change for better health and weight loss. You're reading these pages for a reason, and it is important to examine why you want to make a lifestyle change. In this chapter, we're going to consider both wrong motivations and proper motivations. As part of the proper motivation, we will consider God's vision for why you should make a lifestyle change and look at three reasons to stay motivated.

The various wrong motivations are important to examine. As you consider these different reasons, pause after every paragraph and see if that motivation is your motivation. If it is, then you are almost doomed to continue in your present state. These motivations have one unifying factor—they are temporary and are usually centered on another person.

Perhaps you are headed to a class reunion in a few months. Reunions are notorious for using photos of how we looked in high school on the name badges. How different do you look from that picture taken your senior year in high school? Most of us have changed substantially over the years. Our hairstyles are different as well as our overall physical appearances. You may set weight loss as a goal for this reunion and work toward it. The problem is the motivation is temporary.

Maybe one of your children is getting married in a few months, and you realize that you will be in the wedding pictures. Because of your social role in this situation, you will garner more attention and focus than you have in recent months. You stare down at your midsection and decide it's time to lose some pounds. Again, it's a temporary motivation.

Some husbands try to motivate their wives to lose weight by dangling a financial carrot. They sweetly look at their wives and say, "Honey, if you lose 50 pounds, then you can spend $500 on a new wardrobe." The thought of shopping for new outfits—in smaller sizes—is enticing, but let's look at the message underneath: "You are not OK. You don't look OK, and you would look a lot better if you didn't weigh so much. In fact, I'm backing that idea with my billfold and an investment in your clothes."

Another motivation may be the way others treat you. One of the worst things you can say to an overweight person is "You have a pretty face." What sort of compliment is that? Although it may be the first thing that comes to mind, such a comment is insulting to an overweight person. The real meaning behind those words is "If you would lose weight, you would be a knockout." If you want to compliment an overweight person, then focus on an internal character trait. Don't use their outward appearance as a motivator because the result will be temporary.

Many single people hope to lose weight because they think it will magically transform their social lives. They mistakenly believe that a particular person will ask them for a date or that they will be able to ask a person out if they are slim. Unfortunately, these single individuals are headed for disappointment because this is another improper motivation for shedding pounds.

If you are motivated to lose weight to please someone else—a spouse, a parent, a friend—then what happens when that relationship changes or has a barrier in it? You will return to eating like you have always eaten before.

PROPER MOTIVATIONS

If you are extremely overweight, your goal may be to simply sit in a chair at the movies without bruising your thighs. Or you may want to travel on an airplane without asking a flight attendant for an extender for the seat belt.

You've tried to crack the whip and get those pounds off. It hasn't worked because every motivation that we've examined thus far has been temporary. Let's now look at what we at First Place consider to be proper motivations for successful, permanent weight loss.

Consider a Lifestyle Change

A key emphasis in First Place is a total lifestyle change. We're not looking for the quick solution but a slow and steady process of change. Instead of attempting to lose 30 to 40 pounds in a few weeks, First Place intentionally encourages a loss of one and a half to two pounds per week. If you lose more than that amount, you are losing more than fat and are probably involved in a program that is not nutritionally sound. After the first few weeks of water loss, it is physiologically impossible to lose more than two pounds of fat per week.

Give Your Body to God

Get up and look in the mirror—you may not like what you see. A proper motivation is to give your body to God. You may think, *God isn't interested in my body.* In Romans 12:1,2, the apostle Paul writes,

> Therefore, I urge you, brothers, in view of God's mercy, to offer your bodies as living sacrifices, holy and pleasing to God—this is your spiritual act of worship. Do not conform any longer to the pattern of this world, but be transformed by the renewing of your mind. Then you will be able to test and approve what God's will is—his good, pleasing and perfect will.

We are urged to present our bodies to God as a living sacrifice. The people in the New Testament knew about sacrifice. Every day in the temple, animals were slaughtered and the blood was dripped on the altar as a sacrifice. As a part of our spiritual worship of God, we are called to present our bodies to God. Yes, the Lord cares about our physical bodies. A proper motivation for weight loss and total lifestyle change is to give your body to God. Ask for His transforming power to fill your life. It's a daily process and a key part of our motivation for pleasing God.

First Corinthians 6:19,20 says, "Do you not know that your body is a temple of the Holy Spirit, who is in you, whom you have received from God? You are not your own; you were bought at a price. Therefore honor God with your body." While it's sometimes easy to forget the fact, nonetheless it is true that we have the Spirit of God inside our bodies. As the temples in ancient Corinth housed false gods of stone and wood, Paul used the image of a temple to talk about how God's Spirit lives in our hearts. How are you taking care of your temple?

Sure, our problems in life have not disappeared. We still have financial struggles, problems in our workplace and relational struggles; but our first priority and proper motivation is to turn to God and seek His kingdom. As we put God in first place for our day and with our weight, then everything else falls into place.

Be a Role Model for Others

Another proper motivation for weight loss is to be a leader in your family and a role model for your children and spouse. It is difficult to lead people where you have not been yourself. Many children are overweight and need encouragement from their parents. The weight problems of our children would evaporate if we would lead them by example. When I first started exercising, my oldest granddaughter, Cara, loved to walk or jog with me in the morning for exercise. Would she do it on her own? No way! Yet in a heartbeat, she came with me at my invitation. Children love being with their family. If you can move away from the television set and walk together as a family, it will allow more time for conversation without the interruption of phones and other machines—plus you are working on one of the commitments in First Place: exercise.

Seek Emotional Healing

Weight loss may only be like an emotional Band-Aid. In some cases, you may come to First Place to lose weight when actually those extra pounds are only a symptom of a deeper issue. Women and men who have been emotionally or sexually abused often attempt to hide their pain with food and weight gain. We have offered First Place groups that are specifically for the emotionally damaged. In these particular groups, members follow the First Place meeting schedule and then add an additional hour for deeper sharing. God is interested in every aspect of our lives—including our weight. Unless these people dig down to the deeper issues in their life, their weight loss is like putting a Band-Aid on cancer. It's not enough.

Manage Stress

We live in a high-stress society. Almost every time we turn around, someone asks us to do something else. Our responsibilities pile high at the office, at home and at church. A proper motivation for weight loss is to better manage the stress in life. It's clear to me that as we get our weight, nutrition and exercise under control, our stress level becomes more tolerable. Although I have a stressful job, employee concerns and a heavy travel schedule, I do not suffer from stress. I believe there are four reasons for this:

1. I have a daily quiet time with God each morning when I give the day to Him. He is in charge of my time and schedule.
2. I strive to exercise five days a week. While exercising, I solve problems and plan my day.
3. I am not a worrier. As a child I learned from my mother that the things we worry about never happen. I believe worry is a great stress producer.
4. I get plenty of rest and take time off to play. Rest and leisure time are prerequisites to a stress-free life.

THREE WAYS TO KEEP MOTIVATED

As you start the journey of First Place, it is important to maintain motivation. One of the most common questions our leaders are asked is

"How do you stay motivated?" Here are three steps for staying motivated that have helped me:

1. *Act the way you want to feel.* Zig Ziglar, in his book *See You at the Top*, wrote that it's easier to act your way into a new way of feeling than it is to feel your way into a new way of acting.[1] We need to focus our minds on moving ahead—even when we don't feel like it. I find that this focus will change my feelings about a particular task. For example, some days I don't feel like exercising. A thousand and one excuses crowd into my mind, and if I went with my feelings, I'd just skip it. However, instead of giving in and skipping it, I put on my exercise clothing and get out on the track. My feelings follow my actions. The same is true for any regular discipline, such as having my quiet time each day with the Lord or choosing to eat right: If I take action, then my feelings follow. As you take continuous action for at least 30 days, you develop that action into a habit—whether it is a good action or a bad action. I confess that I don't understand this phenomenon of feeling following action, but from my personal experience, it's true.

2. *Don't be ruled by your feelings.* I know my feelings can't be trusted. One minute I feel great and the next minute I'm upset or angry about something or someone. In *My Utmost for His Highest*, Oswald Chambers wrote:

> There are certain things in life that we need not pray about—moods, for instance. We will never get rid of moodiness by praying, but we will by kicking it out of our lives. Moods nearly always are rooted in some physical circumstance, not in our true inner self. It is a continual struggle not to listen to the moods which arise as a result of our physical condition, but we must never submit to them for a second. We have to pick ourselves up by the back of the neck and shake ourselves; then we will find that we can do what we believed we were unable to do.

The problem that most of us are cursed with is simply that we won't.[2]

Recognize the pitfalls of moods and kick yourself into action, rather than dwell on the negative sensation.

3. *Ask God to help you.* If you are a person who can't stay motivated no matter how hard you try, then go to God, admit your problem and ask for His help. I believe one of the main reasons I stay motivated is my belief in God's wonderful plan for my life. I don't want to miss anything that God has planned.

"Wait a minute," you say. "I don't believe that God has a wonderful plan for my life." Then I challenge you to memorize Jeremiah 29:11 and say it every day until you believe in God's plan. It says, "'For I know the plans I have for you,' declares the LORD, 'plans to prosper you and not to harm you, plans to give you hope and a future.'"

THE ROAD TOWARD SUCCESS

If you keep a positive motivation, it will send you down the road toward success. Some of us have experienced a great deal of success, while others aren't very far down the road. It has been said that success is a journey and not a destination. Here are some ways to ensure success—not just for First Place but in life (note the first letter of each section is based on a letter of the word "success"):

Set a time each day to be alone with God. I like the early mornings because they are less hectic. Psalm 63:1 says: "O God, you are my God, earnestly I seek you; my soul thirsts for you, my body longs for you, in a dry and weary land where there is no water."

Understand that we have no strength on our own but must depend on God's strength in us. Isaiah 40:29 says, "He gives strength to the weary and increases the power of the weak."

Call on God when fear overtakes your heart. Psalm 27:1 says: "The LORD is my light and my salvation—whom shall I fear? The LORD is the stronghold of my life—of whom shall I be afraid?"

Call on your First Place class members or friends for support and encouragement. Ecclesiastes 4:12 says: "Though one may be overpowered, two can defend themselves. A cord of three strands is not quickly broken."

Enjoy the journey. Every day is a gift from God and should be celebrated. Psalm 31:24 says: "Be strong and take heart, all you who hope in the LORD."

Stay in God's Word each day. We need that daily turning to God and the Lord can speak to us through His Word, the Bible. Psalm 119:11 says: "I have hidden your word in my heart that I might not sin against you."

Seek to love God more today than yesterday. Our love for our heavenly Father should be increasing each day. John 14:21 says: "Whoever has my commands and obeys them, he is the one who loves me. He who loves me will be loved by my Father, and I too will love him and show myself to him."

I encourage you to memorize each of the above seven verses from the Bible, so you can stand against the enemy when you are tempted and he whispers in your ear, "You'll never have success." If you are motivated through the power of God's Spirit, you will arrive at the finish line. Philippians 1:6 says, "Being confident of this, that he who began a good work in you will carry it on to completion until the day of Christ Jesus."

Now that we've stirred your motivation, what sort of obstacles and roadblocks will you have to overcome as you seek to change your lifestyle? We'll examine these roadblocks in the next chapter. Let's turn the page and continue the journey.

CHAPTER THREE

OBSTACLES TO OVERCOME

Rhonda Holbrook and her sister, Diana Goodman McDaniel, attended one of our Fitness Week programs several years ago at the Ridgecrest Conference Center. Diana, who appeared for five years on the television show *Hee Haw*, had been sent from her church to learn how to begin a First Place program. But Rhonda wasn't sure why she was attending. At the time, she weighed 238 pounds. Several months before the Fitness Week, Rhonda had a gallbladder attack. At her doctor's suggestion, she had eliminated red meat and sugar from her diet and had managed to lose 25 pounds. "But I was still overeating," Rhonda says.

After eight hours at the Fitness Week, Rhonda was ready to return home. She had difficulty walking around the conference center. When she called her husband, he said, "Darling, why don't you give it a little more time?" During the second day, we divided into prayer groups, and Rhonda was in my small group. Rhonda thought to herself, *Great. Now I'll have to do First Place because I'm in a group with the national director.* As we took prayer requests, Rhonda said, "Carole, I don't know why I'm here this week."

I didn't say anything about her weight but said, "Rhonda, we're glad you've come, and I'm sure God will show you why you are here before the week is over." I didn't know that Rhonda had already tried numerous other programs. She had actually started and stopped one nationally recognized program 15 times—without success.

The next day during the Bible study session, Rhonda felt the Lord speak to her spirit, "When you go back home, Rhonda, I want you to lead the First Place group instead of Diana."

Internally, Rhonda immediately objected and said to the Lord, *I will never be able to take the leadership unless Diana gives me permission without my prompting.* After the class, the two sisters left together. When they stepped through the entryway, Diana turned to Rhonda and said, "The Lord has been speaking to my heart. It's not His will for me to lead the First Place group, but He wants you to do it." Rhonda began to cry at the confirmation from God.

The sisters completed the weeklong program, returned to their local church and met with their pastor. While the First Place program does not require that you be at your goal weight to lead a group, Rhonda's pastor objected to Rhonda's leadership and said, "You have to be an example to lead a weight-loss program." The sisters followed their pastor's leadership and instead agreed to begin the 13-week study program together. They called each other once a week and followed the other eight commitments of First Place. During the first Bible study, Rhonda found one of her three "life verses"—Romans 12:1: "Therefore, I urge you, brothers, in view of God's mercy, to offer your bodies as living sacrifices, holy and pleasing to God—this is your spiritual act of worship." Many times in the past, Rhonda had used this verse to present her life to God. She was amazed to see this verse in the first Bible study of First Place. Rhonda got down on her knees and prayed, "God, I can't do this program on my own, but I'm willing to do what You want."

Rhonda and Diana both lost weight during the 13 weeks. During the first year, Rhonda lost 62 pounds and is currently working to lose 50 more pounds through First Place. After the sisters completed their first 13-week study, their pastor changed his stance and permitted Rhonda to lead a group at the church. The first session involved 12 women; the next had 40 men and women. Ultimately the program grew to several groups that totaled about 80 people. As Rhonda considered the benefits she has received from First Place, she said, "I was already a Christian and walking with the Lord, but I didn't allow God to have anything to do with my weight. Now my life is an open book for a fuller, more intimate relationship with Christ."

DIFFERENT PEOPLE—
DIFFERENT OBSTACLES

Rhonda faced numerous obstacles as she sought to start a First Place program. Your obstacles will be completely different. As you take some initial steps toward a lifestyle change, your mind will cry out with many different excuses. Here we'll examine some common obstacles and consider some ways to overcome them.

"I Don't Have Enough Time"

Time is one of the major excuses used to avoid starting a new program like First Place. You may groan, "I don't have any more hours in my day to exercise or read the Bible. Where will I find the time?"

Each of us has 24 hours in a single day. The question is, Do you use that time wisely? The average American spends 15 hours a week in front of the television set. "Whoa, I don't spend that much time" you might say. One way to judge exactly how much time you spend at the television set is to keep track for a few days. The results may surprise you. We rationalize watching television because of our love for sports or the need to follow the news, yet it takes up a lot of time. You can free up a few more hours in your day if you simply turn off the television set.

Another way to gain more time each day is to set the alarm clock a half hour or an hour earlier. Then use that extra time in a productive fashion. Monday through Friday, I don my exercise clothes and work out with friends before work. I eliminate the excuse of no time by planning this activity as part of my schedule.

God created everything in the world, including time. He has the hours of the day for our schedule—particularly as we turn over those hours into His hands. Solomon wrote about God in the early pages of Ecclesiastes 3:11: "He has made everything beautiful in its time. He has also set eternity in the hearts of men; yet they cannot fathom what God has done from beginning to end." The psalmist says, "This is the day the LORD has made; let us rejoice and be glad in it" (Ps. 118:24). Finally, the apostle Paul encourages us to make good use of our time because the days are evil (see Eph. 5:16).

"I'll Never Be Able to Do It"

Sometimes we look at ourselves and hear a little voice inside that says, *You are a loser. You will never be able to take off those pounds.* This kind of self-talk may have started as a small child when someone in school called you stupid. Instead of responding with a Forrest Gump sort of answer ("Stupid is as stupid does"), you took that message to heart and began to call yourself names. These names and self-talk become another obstacle to your goal of losing weight and changing your lifestyle.

If you have these negative messages spinning in your head (and many of us do), I hope you will open your Bible and remind yourself of God's great love for you. The Lord told the prophet Jeremiah in 31:3, "The LORD appeared to us in the past, saying: 'I have loved you with an everlasting love; I have drawn you with loving-kindness.'"

This truth is only one of the many precious thoughts from God's Word. We need to hold on to these verses when we feel something inside tell us that we are not able to do the First Place program or when we face any other obstacle.

"I Don't Have the Discipline"

Sometimes we chafe at the disciplines involved with First Place. You may look at the nine commitments and instantly conclude, "I don't have the discipline. I admit that I don't have what it takes."

Within the First Place program, you are not alone. As part of a small group, you have other members in your group who can help encourage you in the different disciplines, such as reading your Bible, keeping your Commitment Record or finding time to exercise. Or if you're doing the First Place program with two or three friends, mutual support is going to help you persevere. Many First Place members find encouraging or giving support to fellow members is especially difficult. As a society, we've built relational walls around ourselves to keep people from hurting us because we've been rejected and hurt many times in the past. Through First Place, God wants to bring emotional healing and encourage you in this particular discipline.

Why do we reach out to other people within First Place? Because we learn to love other people with the love that God has shown to us through Christ. I grew up in a generation that believed if people didn't conform to what they were told, they were forgotten. Through reading the Bible, I've learned that God has a totally different perspective. He says that He loves every individual as much as He loves you and me. It is unimportant what they've done or what kind of sin they have committed. In God's eyes, there are no degrees of sin. However, sin separates us from God. In 1 John 1:9,10, God's Word says, "If we confess our sins, he is faithful and just and will forgive us our sins and purify us from all unrighteousness. If we claim we have not sinned, we make him out to be a liar and his word has no place in our lives." When we fail and miss a particular discipline, then we turn to God, ask His forgiveness and try again.

We will not pretend that discipline is easy. It takes a certain type of discipline to attend a weekly meeting, to fill out the Commitment Record with what you eat and to have regular Bible study time. Each of these commitments involves discipline. But what are the results of discipline? Hebrews 12:11 says, "No discipline seems pleasant at the time, but painful. Later on, however, it produces a harvest of righteousness and peace for those who have been trained by it." If you want a harvest of righteousness and peace, then you must follow the course of discipline.

"I'm Afraid I Will Fail"

Fear is a universal problem. It weakens our hearts, robs us of peace of mind and saps our energy. Unfortunately, fear is alive and well in the world of weight loss. Many people are afraid they will fail again after so many previous attempts to lose weight. After they have been in First Place and have reached their goal weight, some people are afraid they will gain back their weight. Leaders of First Place groups are afraid they won't be effective and that members of the group will drop out of the program.

In the Bible, the admonition to "fear not" is used more than 100 times. God knows us well enough to know that we need constant reminders to live in trust and dependence on Him, rather than living in fear and anxiety. I have found several things to be true for my own life, when fears overtake me. Here are four steps to help you overcome your fears:

1. Choose to obey God and leave the consequences of life to Him. Joshua 22:5 says, "But be very careful to . . . love the LORD your God, to walk in all his ways, to obey his commands, to hold fast to him and to serve him with all your heart and all your soul."

2. Recognize that God is greater than your circumstances. Romans 8:31 says, "What, then, shall we say in response to this? If God is for us, who can be against us?"

3. Ask God to make you aware of His presence. In Isaiah 41:10, the prophet wrote, "So do not fear, for I am with you. . . . I will strengthen you and help you; I will uphold you with my righteous right hand."

4. Praise God for delivering you from your fears. Psalm 34:1,4 says, "I will extol the LORD at all times; his praise will always be on my lips. I sought the LORD, and he answered me; he delivered me from all my fears."

Take these four steps into your life and heart as you seek to conquer the obstacle of fear in your life, whether it concerns weight loss or anything else.

NO MATTER THE OBSTACLE—
NO REASON TO QUIT

Some of you today feel like you want to quit. In your mind, you have failed with your weight, and you wonder how you will be able to restore the years ahead. I love the section of the Old Testament where the nation of Israel has sunk low in the eyes of the world. The prophet Joel reminds them of God's words about how He will bring restoration: "I will repay you for the years the locusts have eaten. . . . You will have plenty to eat, until you are full, and you will praise the name of the LORD your God, who has worked wonders for you" (Joel 2:25,26). We need to develop consistency, so we don't quit.

So many times, I have said to our heavenly Father, "I'm in way over my head, Lord. This is too big. When you called me to be involved in First Place, you never told me it was going to be like this." In my own mind, I have tried to have a pity party with God. (Perhaps you've done the same thing with your weight or your relationship with God—you feel like quitting.)

But once again, God reassures me that there is nothing I can't do if He is doing it through me. I must turn away from quitting and refocus on the God of the impossible. He doesn't want me to quit.

One day I heard Ann Landers discuss the results of a survey among parents. To my surprise, many of the parents said that if they had it to do over again, they would never have had children. Those parents wanted to quit, and that attitude is symptomatic of the world in which we live.

Some people say that their reason for quitting is laziness. A lot of times we are lazy about our habits and lifestyle. We tire of doing everything right all the time. Sure we get tired of filling out the Commitment Record and eating all the right foods, but it's not laziness that stops us. It's fear. Underneath everything, we are afraid that if we commit to the First Place program and fail, then people will think less of God. Is God's reputation at stake when we quit? No. God will still be God. Besides, the success is not in the program itself but in the process. The success of the program is a continual dependence on God. We need to give Him first place in our every decision; then in His power we will be able to conquer our fears and concerns.

If fear makes us want to quit, then where does fear come from? Satan is definitely the author of fear. First Peter 5:8 in the *Living Bible* says, "Be careful—watch out for attacks from Satan, your great enemy. He prowls around like a hungry, roaring lion, looking for some victim to tear apart." Notice that the Bible doesn't say that Satan is a lion—only that he acts like one. Let's look at some of the characteristics of a lion. First, lions chase away their own young. In the same way, many of us have been chased away from God before we were fully mature. God wants us to mature in our relationship with Him. This can happen through the First Place program; I've seen it happen in many different people.

Second, a lion attacks sick, young or straggling animals. The enemy knows when we are at our weakest point, so he attacks. When it comes to weight loss, Satan may be whispering to you, "You knew you could never succeed in this program. Why look: you lost 30 pounds and then gained back 10. Why not just quit?" The temptation is to quit the program. However, Matthew 4:23 tells us that Jesus Christ went about healing the sick. If you feel weak or sick, then turn to Jesus; He is strong when we are weak. I draw great encouragement from the passage about Jesus that reads, "For we do not have a high priest who is unable to sympathize with our weaknesses, but we have one who has been tempted in every way, just as we are—yet was without sin" (Heb. 4:15).

The third characteristic of lions is that they choose victims who are alone or not alert. In my own life, I know it is not good for me to be alone. For that reason, I don't keep any food in my home that is a temptation for me. This means that I don't keep any cookies, chocolate candy or ice cream. These are comfort foods for me, so I have learned not to have them readily available. It may be a step of protection that you will also need to take in your own home. As the First Place national director, I'm not going to eat anything in front of you that you shouldn't eat. This means that I ask my husband not to purchase boxes of Girl Scout cookies and slip them into our freezer. I know if those cookies are in my freezer and I'm alone in my home, then Satan will begin to attack. I may deflect the first wave of the attack—determined that I'm not going to give in to those cookies. But if I'm left alone long enough, I'll eat the cookies. I know myself well enough to know that I don't need to be alone with foods that are not the best choices for me. You too will need to consider this type of obstacle in your own life and make some choices about it.

It is important to remember that if you have a personal relationship with Jesus Christ, you are never alone. Jesus says in Hebrews 13:5, "Never will I leave you; never will I forsake you." Satan makes us feel alone, but Jesus is our comforter. When you feel alone, run to Jesus.

The fourth characteristic of a lion is that it hunts at night. The lion is a cowardly creature since he needs the cover of darkness. In the same way, Satan attacks us at night because that's when we are the most vulnerable. We may be tired or sleepy, and our thinking is not as sharp as in the morning when we are refreshed and geared up for the day ahead. Several years ago I took a good friend to a conference, and she received tremendous emotional healing in her life. The night was usually a difficult time for her, but one morning she came to my hotel room with her face glowing. During the night she had latched on to a verse from Psalm 139:12: "Even the darkness will not be dark to you; the night will shine like the day." The daytime and the nighttime are the same to God. We need to stay in the light and run from the darkness.

Finally, a lion patiently stalks its prey with a short, rapid charge. Satan is patient with me and knows how to work on my mind. I used to have a real weakness for Baskin-Robbins ice cream, and there was a shop right down the street from my house. If I went somewhere, I headed down that particular street—whether I had any business there or not. In fact, if I was anywhere near that street, I turned and got on the street that ran past Baskin-Robbins. Before long I would tell myself, *Well, I don't have to stop.* Then my tune changed to, *I may or I may not stop.* In reality, I had already made a decision and it was done: I was stopping at Baskin-Robbins. Because I had entertained the thought, the thought became a reality. Our pastor, in a sermon on temptation, summarized the process: "Temptation; hesitation; participation."

Although your particular weakness will be different from mine, you need to turn control of your weaknesses over into God's capable hands.

Yes, there are many times when I face obstacles in my weight-loss program. I often feel like quitting. That's when I have to remind myself of the story Patsy Clairmont told about her little boy at about age six. Since they lived out in the country, she walked her son to the bus stop. But before she got back to the house, her son had beat her home. She said to him, "What in the world are you doing? The school bus is coming soon."

He looked her straight in the eye and said firmly, "I'm quitting school."

With determination in her eyes, she said, "You can't quit school, and besides, you are only in the first grade. Why are you quitting?"

The boy looked down at the ground and said, "Well, it's too long, it's too hard, and it's boring."

She said, "Son, that's life. Get on the bus."

Sometimes I have to tell this little story to myself. I have to think, *Carole, this is life. Get on the bus.* God didn't promise us that life would be rosy and without difficulty. Instead, the Lord promised to carry us through any situation and any trial. Romans 8:28 says, "And we know that in all things God works for the good of those who love him, who have been called according to his purpose."

As you read about First Place in this book, God knows the obstacles and excuses that you will mount to try and quit. But quitting isn't the answer. Instead, you need to cling even tighter to the hand of God and ask for His strength and enabling in order to walk another step along the journey. He is more than able to accomplish what concerns you today.

In the next chapter, we'll dig deeper into what the Scriptures say about what we eat and our need to be in balance. This spiritual discipline has some unique aspects. Let's turn the page and continue our journey to Christ-centered health.

✳

CHAPTER FOUR

THE SPIRITUAL FOUNDATION

One of Roberta Wasserman's most painful childhood memories involved her weight. In elementary school, every student was herded through a physical. Everyone stood on weight scales in the middle of the gym. When Roberta stepped on the scale, the needle moved past the 100-pound mark. Devastated in front of her peers, Roberta internalized the humiliation of that moment. Her mother took Roberta to Weight Watchers and she did lose weight—but this experience also marked the beginning of many years of self-abuse.

"My weight yo-yoed through my teens," she says. "One small bite of food made me feel too fat, and the distorted body image I saw was unacceptable. Then the deprivation eventually led me to overeat where a thousand bites were not enough." Attending a meeting of Overeater's Anonymous, the other women were shocked that Roberta would attend because she was so "tiny." They were unaware of her struggle with bulimia.

Through Christian therapy, Roberta got in touch with the sad, wounded side of her life and found help for her bulimia disorder. Because she wanted to lose 40 pounds, Roberta joined a First Place group at a local church near her home in Riva, Maryland. Roberta was Christian, but she experienced tremendous growth in her spiritual life through First Place. She says, "First Place got me in touch with the source of the healer of my wounds, my Lord and Savior Jesus Christ. For the first time in my life, I began to write my daily prayers. I read the Bible and the Scriptures came to life."

While in First Place, Roberta lost about 40 pounds, and today she continues in accountable relationships to several group members and keeps the nine commitments. "I've spent a lifetime turning to food, my false god. With the help of First Place, I've gradually come to realize that I can stare at my open pantry and know there will never be enough food to satisfy my soul, because only the Lord can meet that need." In First Place, Roberta has gained a treasured relationship with Jesus Christ.

BACK TO BASICS

Several years ago I had a bulging disc in my neck. This physical ailment returned me to the basics in my emotional, mental, physical and spiritual life. My hurting neck landed me in bed for several weeks and eventually led to physical therapy.

For many years, I had resisted any sort of weight training. When I started the First Place program, I began to walk and then jog. I loved jogging, but I despised strapping into a weight machine and lifting weights. Yet the physical therapy for my neck involved weights. After several weeks of therapy, I began to think, *Hey, I don't need to go to physical therapy to do these exercises. We've got the same machines at our church workout room, and I can do it on my own.*

For years, people had seen me jogging on the track at our church with friends, and one man in particular had been encouraging me to lift weights. I never made any pretense about lifting weights; I was not going to start it. When this man saw me begin in the weight room after my neck injury, he laughed and said, "Carole, I've been after you for three years to do some strength training on your upper body." It took my neck pain to return me to the basics. I now know that as long as I stretch, exercise and lift weights, I don't have any pain. But if I quit my exercises for a week or two, then the pain returns in my neck. I have to stick with the basics.

I'm one of the few people you will meet who absolutely loves to exercise. Several years ago my husband, Johnny, and I went to the Smokey Mountains for a week. We loved the gorgeous October weather and enjoyed hiking in the forests as the leaves were turning their brilliant colors. One morning we packed a lunch and hiked two and a half miles each way to a waterfall. On the way up to the waterfall, I crossed a small bridge and the bottom step was wet. My tennis shoe turned and my foot twisted, tearing some ligaments in my ankle. My injury was made worse because I had to walk over two miles to get assistance. The injury put a halt to my jogging for six months. After not jogging for six months, it was like starting over again—I had to return to the basics. Although I bristle when I have to begin again, this is a very real part of life.

One of my friends, Chris, saw my reaction at starting over and said, "Carole, starting over is a basic part of any recovery. In Alcoholics Anonymous they tell you to take one day at a time." When you, the reader, look at your weight situation, you may feel totally out of control. You need to return to the basics in order to understand your spiritual foundation.

BIBLICAL BASICS

The First Place program isn't built on a theory or a premise but on the solid truth that has stood the test of the ages—the Bible. The Bible says a great deal about everything in life. Its pages are inspired and have the absolute authority to teach us how to live to the fullest. Before we examine First Place in detail, let's consider what God says about His plan and desires.

First, when it comes to the physical aspects of life, our bodies are the temples of the Holy Spirit. If you have asked Jesus Christ to come into your life as your Savior, then God's Spirit lives in you. Paul reminded the church at Corinth about this fact when he said, "Do you not know that your body is a temple of the Holy Spirit, who is in you, whom you have received from God? You are not your own; you were bought at a price. Therefore honor God with your body" (1 Cor. 6:19,20). It is our spiritual obligation to honor God with our physical bodies. You may not like the current shape of your physical body; that is why you have turned to First Place. As you follow the First Place program, you are improving your physical temple where God's Spirit lives. You can feel good about the fact that you are improving your body.

Balance and moderation are also basic spiritual tenets that are reinforced repeatedly in the Scriptures. Consider for a moment the life of the Lord Jesus when He walked the face of the earth. The apostle Luke tells us in Luke 2:52 (TLB): "So Jesus grew both tall [physical] and wise [mental], and was loved by God [spiritual] and man [emotional]." Jesus had a sense of balance in His life. Yet besides the example of Christ's life, He also encouraged us to have balance. When Jesus was asked about the greatest commandment for man, He said, "'Love the Lord your God with all your heart [emotional] and with all your soul [spiritual] and with all your strength [physical] and with all your mind' [mental]; and, 'Love your neighbor as yourself'" (Luke 10:27).

Besides balance, the Scriptures also exhort us to live in moderation. Overeating, overdrinking or any type of excessive behavior is not pleasing to God. Paul wrote the church, "Let your moderation be known unto all men. The Lord is at hand" (Phil. 4:5, KJV).

If we obey God's desire for our lives and maintain our sense of balance, then we can enjoy the spiritual, emotional, mental and physical blessings of God. God honors our obedience with His blessing. As the psalmist wrote in Psalm 103:2-5, "Praise the LORD, O my soul, and forget not all his benefits—who forgives all your sins and heals all your diseases; he redeems your life from the pit and crowns you with love and compassion, who satisfies your desires with good things so that your youth is renewed like the eagle's."

These words of the psalmist encourage us to celebrate God's benefits and to obey the words of Scripture. Isaiah tells us that we will have peace from God as we follow the Scriptures: "This is what the LORD says—your Redeemer, the Holy One of Israel: 'I am the LORD your God, who teaches you what is best for you, who directs you in the way you should go. If only you had paid attention to my commands, your peace would have been like a river, your righteousness like the waves of the sea'" (Isa. 48:17,18).

The Bible even has a few words of wisdom about too much food consumption: "When you sit to dine with a ruler, note well what is before you, and put a knife to your throat if you are given to gluttony. Do not crave his delicacies, for that food is deceptive. For drunkards and gluttons become poor, and drowsiness clothes them in rags" (Prov. 23:1-3, 21).

THE VALUE OF GETTING BACK TO BASICS

It's tiresome to keep going back to the basics. In First Place, we are always starting over again. Before I know it, it's time to join another 13-week group. Maybe you joined a group and didn't find any success during those 13 weeks. Why do it again? For me, the reason to repeat is found in Romans 8:29, where Paul writes, "For those God foreknew he also predestined to be conformed to the likeness of his Son, that he might be the firstborn among many brothers." God has a purpose when we have to start over again. That purpose is to cause us to look more like His Son, Jesus Christ. As we return to the basics, then God can mold us into the people that He wants.

The woodcarver looks at a block of wood and sees a beautiful carved wooden duck inside that block. God looks at our outsides and sees that through the carving process, we too can be made into beautiful creations. It's like God says to us, "If you will not quit, then I will do My work in your life." In the First Place program, success is found in the process or the journey.

Start First Place

There are three basics that will take you into a deeper relationship with God and Jesus Christ. First, you need to *start First Place*. Our own office staff participates in the 13-week First Place program. This last session they lost a total of 121 pounds and everyone turned in a weekly Commitment Record. We stayed on the Live-It program every week and each of us lost weight. Is it amazing? No, we know our program works, and it works because in the process, God blesses us with success. Although we sometimes want someone else to do the work, only we can do the work of First Place. It can't be done by anyone else. Even our staff knows the value of starting over. God is the God of "beginning again."

When my ankle was hurt, a stationary bike was all I could do to continue my exercise program. Some mornings I would wake up and think, *I don't want to get on that stationary bike for my exercise. In fact, I hate that thing because it doesn't go anywhere and I have to just sit there.* Still, I had to begin again.

For me, exercise is an appointment that I made many years ago, and I still show up for that appointment five times each week. When I'm at home, I go down to the track at the church and exercise with my friends. If I'm not there, people will ask me, "What happened to you today, Carole?" Of course, I don't always feel like going; but when I show up, God always meets me there. Invariably on some of my worst days, I'll be exercising and somebody will show up that I have not seen in a long time. We will exercise together and begin sharing what the Lord has done in our lives. The exercise time flies by; I don't want it to end because I know that the Lord brought that particular person to me that day.

I always have plenty of excuses when I don't want to exercise. However, I've found that when I feel sluggish and am not anxious to exercise, that's when I must push myself out to go ahead and do it anyway. Somewhere along the way, my attitude changes and the exercise becomes enjoyable. Zig Ziglar says that if you want anything to become a habit, you need to do it for at least 21 days without missing a day.[1]

People have told me how they had exercised regularly for three years and then they suddenly quit for two weeks because of sickness or some other problem. Before they knew it, a year had passed without regular exercise. Bad habits are easy to accumulate, but they can be broken with a fresh start.

One of the commitments in First Place is to fill out a Commitment Record with all of the food that you have eaten. I've been filling out CRs since 1981. Sometimes I go through this mental process: *This isn't so bad. I can have that type of food if I want. I'll cut back a little bit later.* Or I'll think,

I've had a hard day and I need to eat this. I'll do better tomorrow. If I continue to go down the road with this kind of thinking, what happens? One bad day gets added to another bad day. That is why in the First Place program if you eat something that is not loaded with nutrition—like a candy bar or a piece of pie—you put that item on your CR anyway. Then for your next meal, you start again on the First Place program. You forget about the food choice that wasn't very nutritious, and eat good nutrition the next meal. When you do this, your mind and your emotions acknowledge that you made an unwise choice for weight loss, but you begin all over again the very next meal. You want to avoid thinking, *Oh, I ate something that I wasn't supposed to eat. I'll skip my next meal and do better tonight.* That way of thinking will lead to bingeing by nightfall. Then after bingeing, you'll believe you've blown the program for the entire week and tailspin into a major stall. Remember, the first basic principle is to always begin again.

Learn How to Fail
The second basic principle is to *learn how to fail*. Some of us do not know how to fail gracefully. You have to be willing to risk failure if you are going to do anything significant in life. Thomas Edison failed thousands of times before he invented the electric lightbulb. I can't see many of us failing thousands of times before we quit. Instead, we would give up early and say, "Well, that just isn't meant to be." Someone once asked Thomas Edison about all of his failures and he said, "I have learned a lot of ways not to do something."

Tim Hansel, in his book *Holy Sweat*, tells the story of a young man starting his job as the new president of a bank. The new president went to the retiring president and said, "I need to ask you a question."

The older, distinguished gentleman looked up and the younger man asked, "What is it that makes you a success?"

The man smiled and said, "Two words—'good decisions.'"

The young man said, "Oh, thank you." And he walked out of the room, but in a minute he came back puzzled and said, "Sir, I need to ask another question. How do you make good decisions?"

The older gentleman looked up from his desk and said, "One word—'experience.'"

"Oh, thank you, sir," said the young man and walked out of the room, but almost immediately he returned.

The older bank president put his pen down and looked up. The younger man asked, "How do you get that experience?"

"Two words—'bad decisions.' "[2]

In my life, I have learned some of my most valuable lessons from bad decisions. Don't be afraid of failing. If you are afraid to fail, you will miss some of the most valuable lessons of life. Paul talked about this process in Romans 7:19,20: "For what I do is not the good I want to do; no, the evil I do not want to do—this I keep on doing. Now if I do what I do not want to do, it is no longer I who do it, but it is sin living in me that does it." Many times we fail because of sin in our lives, but God takes us right back through that failure to teach us lessons that would not be learned through any other manner.

God gives us a lot of rope in our lives. Although I deserve a lot of judgment from God, He continually shows me mercy. He gives me a long rope but eventually pulls it in and asks, "Are you convinced now that you cannot do a better job than I can do?" God knows that we must realize our failures, so we will lean more heavily on His power in our lives.

In the area of weight loss, you may have failed many times. Give that failure into God's hands, saying, "I have proven to You that I'm a failure. I cannot do this. I cannot lose weight. Even if I do lose weight, I always gain it back. I'm a failure." The Lord has been waiting for you to reach this decision point, and He will respond, "You are not going to be a failure anymore; because if you let me do it, I'll do it." Through the commitments in First Place, we learn that failure is never fatal. We also learn that when we do fail, we simply give that failure to God and begin again.

Persevere

The third and final basic point is to *persevere*. The apostle Paul knew about perseverance and wrote the Philippian church, "I press on toward the goal to win the prize for which God has called me heavenward in Christ Jesus" (Phil. 3:14). Paul exhorted us to keep moving toward our goals despite any obstacles we might experience.

Have you ever prayed for patience? The Bible tells us that we get patience through tribulation. Sometimes I'd like to ignore Romans 5:3 (*TLB*), which says, "We can rejoice, too, when we run into problems and trials [and everyone has problems and trials] for we know that they are good for us—they help us learn to be patient." That Scripture alone is enough to convince me never to pray for patience. I've got enough problems and trials in my life without asking God to send more. Instead, we need to learn how to persevere, because it has been said that perseverance is patience plus endurance.

Perseverance also is a gift from God that reminds us of our options. Yes, we can quit. I've quit for months at a time, but God always draws me back. Many times I want to quit when the Holy Spirit is dealing with an area of my life that I am unwilling to change. I don't want to deal with it, so I draw back. In fact, I've sometimes done this for as long as six weeks, but God keeps after me to return. When I finally return to God's everlasting arms, I think, *Why did I waste six weeks?* Those feelings of peace don't come until I obey with my mind and my will. As I said in an earlier chapter, actions never follow feelings, but feelings always follow actions. Perseverance has nothing to do with feelings but everything to do with our continual relationship with Jesus Christ.

Tim Hansel included the following poem, *The Paradoxes of Man,* by Philip Brewer, in his book *Holy Sweat*:

Strong enough to be weak.
Successful enough to fail.
Busy enough to take time.
Wise enough to say, "I don't know."
Serious enough to laugh.
Rich enough to be poor.
Right enough to say, "I'm wrong."
Compassionate enough to discipline.
Conservative enough to give freely.
Mature enough to be childlike.
Righteous enough to be a sinner.
Important enough to be last.

Courageous enough to fear God.

Planned enough to be spontaneous.

Controlled enough to be flexible.

Free enough to endure captivity.

Knowledgeable enough to ask questions.

Loving enough to be angry.

Great enough to be anonymous.

Responsible enough to play.

Assured enough to be rejected.

Stable enough to cry.

Victorious enough to lose.

Industrious enough to relax.

Leading enough to serve.[3]

The Bible is full of paradoxes. Jesus says that if you want to have something, then you have to give it away. If you want to be strong, then you have to be weak. If you want to find the scriptural foundation for our Christ-centered health program, then you need to return to the basics. You must begin again, learn to fail and never give up.

One of the keys to First Place is finding balance. We will explore this concept in the next chapter. Let's continue the journey.

*

DISCOVERING
BALANCE

For more than 20 years Terry Dollar, from Marion, Indiana, was overweight and could feel her emotions spiraling out of control. By the end of 1995, the doctor gave Terry a diagnosis of severe depression and anxiety. The next month her depression increased because her grandmother died and the chemotherapy her only sister Becky was receiving was not working. Because of her poor concentration, Terry lost her job; she then began caring for her sister. Terry's eating habits came into focus on Valentine's Day at Becky's home. Terry finished off a one-pound box of chocolate and was almost unaware that she had eaten it. Becky became upset, and in a dying wish, asked her sister to lose weight. Terry lost her sister to cancer on February 23.

That spring a First Place program was started at her church, and Terry joined the group. At the first meeting she weighed in at 284 pounds, almost twice what her 5-foot, 8-inch frame should carry. After a year in the program, Terry had lost 133 pounds and was within 10 pounds of her goal weight. Yet from her perspective, First Place has done much more than help her achieve weight loss.

Twenty-five years earlier Terry had become a Christian, but she had never turned control of her life over to Jesus in any real sense. Before starting First Place, Terry vowed never to diet again because it was too difficult and she always gained back more than she lost. She says, "For Becky's sake, I gave First Place the last chance and told the Lord, 'I know my weight is a poor witness for You; it's killing my knees and most likely me. So if it's Your will that I lose weight, You'll have to do the bulk of the work. I turn it all over to You.'"

God honored Terry's prayer and took over. Since her involvement in the First Place program, her depression is gone, she has more energy, and her knees don't hurt. Terry explains the changes in her life by saying, "He has given me a stronger faith in Him, and I have truly given Him first place in my life. I know Becky is with God in heaven cheering me on."

LIFE OUT OF CONTROL

Sometimes our lives whirl out of control. In your life, perhaps your consumption of food is out of control. Or possibly a relationship has suddenly been broken in your family or among your friends. Maybe your work has piled so high that it is out of control. For many years I loved reading good novels, and this area of my life got out of control. In the early 1980s, my mother took my sister and me on a trip through Austria. I had never been to that part of the world. At the airport, before boarding the plane, our minister of music, who was traveling with us, recommended that I buy a copy of *The Thornbirds* to read during the trip. While traveling through some of the most panoramic scenery in the world, I had my eyes glued to the printed page of that novel. I read that thick book in the back of the bus throughout Austria. Occasionally I would stray from my novel when someone said, "Oh, that's beautiful." I looked out the windows, saw it quickly and returned to my novel. My reading habits had whirled out of control, and I was stuck in *The Thornbirds* while missing Austria.

Other times my life gets out of control in the area of relationships. Sometimes things start out right and then turn upside down. A while back we eliminated cable television from our home. We had basic cable and determined that it wasn't worth what it cost us and should be eliminated—even the minimum service. Our lack of cable television posed a bit of a problem for my husband (who had decided to get rid of it). Johnny has never been a good sleeper, and when he wakes up in the middle of the night and has trouble sleeping, he turns on the television. We laughed about taking away his pacifier.

The next morning when I kissed him good-bye, I asked, "Did you sleep well?"

He smiled and said, "I really did sleep well last night."

The truth was, I had slept well for the first time in quite a while because Johnny wasn't awake watching television throughout the night. As I left for work, I had a warm feeling toward Johnny. After several hours in my office, I thought I would call him just to chat. On our phone, we have call waiting, but Johnny hates to use this convenience. When I called, he was on the phone, and it took about eight rings before he answered it. With every single ring he heard, I learned later, Johnny had grown more uptight. Finally he managed to push the right button and said an exasperated, "Hello."

I said, in a cheery voice, "Just me."

He abruptly said, "Well, I'll have to call you back. I'm on the other line." He hung up, and I stepped out of my office to get an apple. While I was gone, Johnny called me back. My assistant said, "She'll be back in a few minutes."

When Johnny called back a second time, he said, "Well, what did you want? I was on the phone." Well, you know that warm feeling that I had had a few minutes earlier? It evaporated.

I said to him, "I didn't really want anything in particular. I just wanted to see how you were doing. You know, we didn't get to talk much this morning." After a few more minutes, our conversation ended. My warm feeling for Johnny had disappeared, and I wanted that feeling back instead of the confusion. It seemed like the circumstances of my day were going into a tailspin. What had started as a warm fuzzy had ended as a cold lumpy.

When I feel like circumstances are spiraling downward in my life, God has taught me that whether I'm right side up or upside down, I need to turn those circumstances over to Him. He is the only one who can bring balance into my life.

BALANCE IN EVERY ASPECT OF LIFE

The First Place program is designed to bring balance to every area of life: mental, physical, spiritual and emotional. Since the First Place food plan is not a diet but a way of life, we encourage every participant to begin with a willingness to change his or her lifestyle in a variety of areas for balance and personal growth. We accomplish this lifestyle change through completing, to the best of our ability, the nine commitments that are detailed in the next two chapters. Most of us will not be able to accomplish every one of the nine commitments every day. Nonetheless, we strive for this goal because, if reached, it will bring balance to our lives. Our heavenly Father has a single-minded purpose: to conform us to the image of His Son, Jesus. In the *New Living Translation*, Romans 8:29 says, "For God knew his people in advance, and he chose them to become like his Son, so that his Son would be the firstborn, with many brothers and sisters." Did you catch the significance of that verse? God selected us to become like Jesus. For this process to take place, God wants to change us in every area of life.

Through First Place you will be involved in a plan that incorporates the four major areas of life: mental, physical, spiritual and emotional. The changes in each area of your life can be quite dramatic. Frequently I meet men and women who initially joined the First Place program with weight loss as their main goal. After they reach their weight-loss goal, these same people say the spiritual changes have been the most significant changes in their lives. As God receives His rightful position in our lives, many unexpected blessings occur. Matthew 6:33 (KJV) tells us, "Seek ye first the kingdom of God, and his righteousness; and all these things shall be added unto you." In the pages that follow, we will examine each of the four areas and explore why balance is important in each one.

MENTAL

Do not conform any longer to the pattern of this world, but be transformed by the renewing of your mind. Then you will be able to test and approve what God's will is—his good, pleasing and perfect will (Rom. 12:2).

For most of us, when it comes to using our mind, we are just plain lazy. We only use a fraction of the mental capacities that God has given us. As we grow older, if we don't stay mentally active, we begin to lose brain power.

In First Place, we are challenged to think and use our mental capabilities in several ways.

Learn Scripture

Each week we memorize one verse of Scripture and recite it when we weigh in at our meeting. I encourage you to practice this memory verse with a friend or family member if you are not participating in a group. Since I have been using our Scripture memory CDs and audiocassettes since they were introduced in the fall of 2000, I have been able to memorize 50 verses. Having been in First Place for 20 years, you would think that I would have memorized all 80 of the memory verses. Well, learning a verse and reciting it when I get on the scale are quite different from learning the verse and incorporating it into my life. For the last few months, I have been meeting a friend each morning and while we walk side by side on treadmills, we practice our memory verses. By listening to the CD while driving, saying the verses each morning and learning to pray the verses, I am making these verses a vital part of my life. Initially you may scoff at memorizing a single verse from the Bible. If you stay in the program for one year, you will have memorized 40 Bible verses, one for each week of four 10-week Bible studies. In First Place we also read and study our Bibles and then discuss our Bible study at our weekly meeting. I have found that if I don't have regular Bible study in a group, I tend to grow lax when I study on my own initiative. Last summer, because of my intense travel schedule, I wasn't in a regular study group. I decided to be independent and purchase a Kay Arthur Bible study at my Christian bookstore, so I could study on my own. At the end of the summer, I had not completed the first week. I believe each of us is more effective when we are accountable to others in some sort of a small group.

Use Your "Dead Time"

Maybe you don't feel like you have any "dead time," but each of us has some space in our day that has nothing going on—in the car, waiting in a doctor's office, standing in line at the supermarket and so on. In First Place, we use these empty moments to listen, read, memorize or study.

In the Houston area, we have a lot of dead time driving across town because of frequent traffic jams. In 1985, I decided that I needed to fill this time with things of God, and tapes appeared to be a perfect solution. However, tapes of Scripture, Christian music or motivational talks were not a luxury I felt that I could afford at that time. I mentioned the idea in my First Place meeting, and the next week, a woman in my class arrived with a grocery bag full of cassettes. She explained, "I want you to have these tapes. My husband and I have been to every seminar that comes to town. These tapes are from motivational speakers, and I don't need you to return them. Please listen to them; then give them to others." I followed her advice and still listen to cassettes of sermons or motivational talks when I exercise or drive in my car.

Today First Place offers a set of audiocassettes and CDs that contains our memory verses set to music. Each set of 10 verses is on a separate cassette prepared by Rick Crawford and Jeff Nelson. Listening to the catchy tunes accompanying the Scriptures will stimulate your own mental activity. At first, it may seem hard; but as you practice, the cassettes become a way of life. I have found that the more I know and learn, the more my desire to know and learn grows.

Avoid Negative Thinking

I believe that the mind is the most significant player in our quest for emotional stability. A number of people who enter the First Place program suffer from emotional abuse, both from others in the past and also from negative thinking that they heap on themselves. Zig Ziglar calls this "stinkin' thinkin'." Do you have these sorts of mental messages in your mind?

They could be something like, *I'll never lose that weight. It took me years to get here. I've lost a few pounds before and gained it right back. Why will this be different?*

Or perhaps you tell yourself, *See how stupid that sounded. I'm not even capable of putting together a coherent sentence. What business do I have saying anything in a small group?* Your particular messages may be completely different, but whatever they are, they spring into your mind uninvited. Whenever you have a bad week, this negative thinking overtakes your emotions and you come to class feeling hopeless and depressed. No one is immune; it can happen to participants and leaders alike.

In June 1997, I had shoulder surgery; for six weeks my only exercise was during my physical therapy sessions three times a week. In my mind, I rationalized that a regular workout schedule was impossible, so I planned to wait until my therapy concluded before starting my regular exercise again. Actually, I *had* exercised during this six-week period—at the two First Place Fitness Weeks at the Ridgecrest and Glorieta Conference centers. I thought I needed to be a role model for our participants in the area of exercise. Still, my mind had just convinced my emotions that it would be better to wait until I felt like exercising voluntarily before I resumed my regular exercise schedule.

During this time I went through a sort of transformation in this area of my life. I began to dwell on the aches and pains of my shoulder until I was depressed. Hopeless feelings washed over me; I thought I would never be whole again. One Monday, after several weeks of my strange behavior, my assistant, Pat Lewis, said to me, "Carole, is something else wrong, or is it just your shoulder bothering you?"

Quickly I answered, "Nothing else is wrong, Pat. It's just my shoulder." Yet I continued to think about her question all afternoon. As I thought about it, I understood that my physical condition was consuming my thoughts—day and night. During the night hours, I hadn't been able to sleep well because I woke up every time I turned over. During the day, I constantly assessed my physical condition: was it better, or worse? Suddenly I understood that because I had given up my exercise routine, the balance of my life had become upset.

The next morning I began my normal routine—as it had been before the surgery. I got up, had my quiet time and left home so that I arrived at the gym by 6:00 A.M. I had a great workout and, to my amazement, a wonderful day. For the first time in six weeks, I felt energized and enthusiastic. My newfound knowledge about myself brought such excitement that on Wednesday I went to the gym at 5:30 A.M., so I could keep my 7:15 physical therapy appointment. I felt my therapy would go better than it had in the past. And I was right. I walked into the session and when asked "How are you feeling?" I said "Great," instead of my usual "Oh, maybe a little better." Everything looked different and brighter than it had on Monday. What was the difference?

Nothing radical had changed with my shoulder; it still needed time to heal. The difference was mental—a changed mind about my condition. I determined to do what I could do and leave the rest to God. Feelings always follow actions, and actions follow a change of mind.

Enlarge Your Vocabulary

Another way to challenge yourself in the mental area is to learn a new word to increase your vocabulary each week. At our group of Christian Life Communicators (a sort of Christian version of a Toastmasters speaking group), we learn a new word each week. The person in charge of the meeting selects a word that very few of us know, and then we use that new word whenever we speak at the meeting. The challenge is to work the word into natural, everyday conversation. Anyone can do this activity. Just add new words into your vocabulary each week, and then use those new words in daily conversation. Some of us are so saturated in our regular word choice that we rarely say anything exciting. This exercise will help stretch your mental powers.

Read Regularly

Begin to read on a regular basis and it will increase your mental capacity. I tend to be an all-or-nothing sort of person. If I can't sit down and read an entire book, then I won't pick it up and read part of it. Yet if you read for only 20 minutes every day, after a year you will have read 20 200-page books. I find that amount of reading remarkable. Each of us can take a chunk of time and read for 20 minutes. A regular reading program would improve the mental aspects of our life. During the last year I have made it a habit to read for at least 30 minutes each night before I go to sleep. I have been able to read some wonderful biographies of great Christian heroes, which helps to increase my faith.

If you are a poor reader or you don't retain what you read, consider this alternative: begin listening to the Scripture memory cassettes or

CDs mentioned earlier. If I wake up during the night, I find the words to these verses playing through my mind. You, too, can be mentally stimulated as you saturate yourself by listening to God's Word. Many wonderful books are also available on audiocasettes.

Years ago, when First Place began, we didn't put as much emphasis on the mental aspect of the program as we do today. Medical professionals continually stress the importance of using our minds as we age. We have been encouraged to do crossword puzzles to keep our minds active. I believe in First Place we have found a tool much more valuable than a crossword puzzle. The addition of the Scripture memory songs to the First Place program has proven to us how much our minds are capable of remembering. My assistant's daughter-in-law homeschools her children. The other day the children called Pat and sang 1 Peter 5:8 to her on the phone. Their mom said that they had easily memorized the verse on the CD just from listening in the car!

We can't ignore the fact that mental growth can have a profound influence on how successfully we handle the complexities of life. Some say "the battle is won or lost in the mind." When we give Christ Jesus first place in our minds, He can do anything with our lives.

PHYSICAL

So whether you eat or drink or whatever you do, do it all for the glory of God (1 Cor. 10:31).

The second area of our lives that needs to be in balance is the physical. The four components of balance in this area are proper nutrition, exercise, rest and stress management. Within First Place, we primarily focus on proper nutrition and exercise. The body is a wonderful creation that wants to heal itself. If people receive proper nutrition and exercise, most will find more energy than they have had in years. Regular exercise not only helps you sleep better, but it is also a great stress reliever.

Years ago, everyone raised his or her own meat, fruits and vegetables. The food was nutritious, and people had to exert physical energy to get it from the seed stage to the table. In First Place, we ask our members to eat food in as close to its natural state as possible. By "natural state," we mean foods that are fresh, whole and pure. We try to avoid processed foods because they are loaded with preservatives and sodium.

The primary physical motivation behind the First Place program is to develop and maintain a healthy body that can serve God as long as possible. The quantity of our life doesn't mean much when there is no quality, so our primary interest is not just getting thinner. Many thin people have high body fat, making them walking time bombs for a variety of diseases. It is wonderful to be thin if low body fat and lots of lean mass accompany it.

Many people start the First Place program to lose weight, but many others begin because of a health problem such as heart disease, high blood pressure or diabetes. Numerous young couples begin so that their children will eat nutritiously; they realize their children would otherwise simply follow their poor example. Through First Place, a participant is educated about nutrition, so it becomes obvious that he or she needs to make a lifestyle change. Our primary physical difficulty is not losing weight but gaining weight. Anyone can lose weight, but most of the time we regain it before we have had those new clothes cleaned three times.

Through the First Place program, you will not find quick weight loss. Most people who lose weight quickly soon return to their old ways of eating and gain back the weight. Through a lifestyle change, participants achieve balance in the physical area of their lives. Most people who join any weight-loss program think, *When can I stop doing this and eat what I used to eat?* Unless our lifestyle changes, we are doomed to the same patterns of failure. When you give Christ first place in your life, He can bring about true change. As you admit to the Lord that you are powerless to change yourself, God steps in and begins to change you. Although many people experience dramatic physical changes (as you've already read about in earlier chapters of this book), in the long run, most of the participants in First Place say that the most important changes are in the spiritual aspects of their lives.

We want these physical changes because we know that "man looks at the outward appearance, but the LORD looks at the heart" (1 Sam. 16:7).

As we look inside ourselves with God's perspective, we see our own misery. If we are overweight, we also know that anyone else we meet sees a body where God obviously does not have full control. Every sin is equal in God's sight, but the sin of gluttony is worn like a walking advertisement.

As you learn to eat right with a low-fat diet that is very low in sugar, you must also exercise. If you don't participate in these two physical acts, then you will pay the price. Before I began an exercise program, I used to come home from work and lay on the sofa for an hour before I could even think about making dinner.

One woman in my First Place class had a brother suddenly drop dead from a heart attack at age 48. Many of you reading this book probably discount this experience for yourselves and think, *It will never happen to me.* Or if it does, then you will have angioplasty or heart bypass surgery. Unfortunately, most people's ideas about heart attacks aren't based on reality. The most common symptom of a heart attack is sudden death. This man who suddenly died of a heart attack was a walking time bomb: he was a chain smoker who didn't eat right or exercise. Each of us has the opportunity to change our lives and begin an exercise program, but we have to do it for the right motivation. Our primary motivation should not be for more energy or to avoid a heart attack but to please God with our bodies.

In my life, balance in the physical area is the hardest to achieve and maintain. Everyone has a lifetime of habits, which comprise who we are as people. When we face times of stress, loneliness, boredom, anger or even joy and celebration, we automatically revert to our old habits. Only God can retrain our minds and emotions and thus retrain our bodies.

My solution for balance in the physical area is to continually make little changes and to have the mental determination not to return to the old way. For instance, several years ago, I quit eating bacon; and now I am no longer tempted to eat bacon. In my life, the turning point for bacon consumption came one day when my husband said, "You know we probably shouldn't eat anything that will keep in the refrigerator for months."

Another part of the physical area that has been difficult for me is getting the milk that my body needs. I have never enjoyed drinking milk, so I struggled to get this nutrition for a long time. I've discovered I like yogurt, and I also enjoy milk shakes made with frozen fruit. So for my milk consumption, I keep yogurt and fresh fruit readily available in my home.

Through the First Place program, you are never forced to eat foods you hate. Every exchange list or serving list contains foods you do like and you may select these foods. Since 1981, I have been living the First Place program and the changes to my eating habits have been gradual. This program will never make a real difference in your life until you transfer head knowledge to the heart. We each have enough head knowledge to eat healthy foods, but only time will change our feelings about these foods. From my perspective, First Place is a lifelong program that over the passage of time gives balance in every area of life. We must be patient and not quit before we achieve this balance. Our heavenly Father is extremely patient and merciful with us. Therefore, shouldn't we be patient and merciful with ourselves? All true change takes time, yet time is what we resist so vigorously.

Our society wants instant everything. It will take time for God to teach us everything about a balanced life. True success is in the process—not the program. When we give Christ control of our physical bodies, we must ultimately surrender our fleshly desires. Our bodies naturally want their own way. Paul said it best in 1 Corinthians 9:26,27: "Therefore I do not run like a man running aimlessly; I do not fight like a man beating the air. No, I beat my body and make it my slave so that after I have preached to others, I myself will not be disqualified for the prize."

SPIRITUAL

But seek first his kingdom and his righteousness, and all these things will be given to you as well (Matt. 6:33).

These words from Jesus are the foundational words for the First Place program. The spiritual aspect of the program is the third crucial area. It is only when we give Christ first place in every area of our lives that He can reveal His plans for us and make us into His image. Maybe you are saying to yourself, *Well, when it comes to my life, God has His work cut out for Him.* Trust me, no job is too big for God. Your responsibility is to release your own will and give God control.

When I was 12, Jesus Christ became my Savior, and I became a Christian. Regretfully it wasn't until 30 years later that Jesus became Lord of my life. There were multiple reasons why Jesus was not Lord, but the bottom line was that I wanted to retain control of my own life. While I retained complete control of my life, I tied God's hands. He was always in my life, helping me in my marriage and in raising our children, but He didn't have the freedom to do His complete work in my life until I released my control.

This spiritual issue of control remains a mystery to me, yet from the evidence in my life since 1984, I wish I had turned it over sooner. My favorite Scripture is Jeremiah 29:11: "'For I know the plans I have for you,' declares the LORD, 'plans to prosper you and not to harm you, plans to give you hope and a future.'"

I can almost guarantee that the spiritual changes that result from the First Place program will be the most meaningful in your life. From my years in First Place, I have heard many weight-loss testimonies. In each case, the person is quick to say that the weight loss is great, but the spiritual changes are greater. God knows that we are created to bring honor and glory to Him. Until we fulfill that destiny, we can never live balanced lives.

In the First Place program, we achieve a spiritual balance by starting every day with reading our Bible. Each day we also answer several Bible study questions that only take a few minutes to complete. Everyone who participates in First Place learns what it means to have a quiet time and pray each day. In the beginning, you may only spend a few minutes in prayer, but as you grow in your understanding of God's love for you and His desire to spend time with you, your prayer time will become longer and more meaningful. The entire First Place program is designed to take bite-sized pieces of time every day. It does not require hours of your time. When you understand that the nine commitments are for your good, you will want to continue each commitment in order to experience the benefits and changes that lead to a lifetime of good health.

An improved emphasis on prayer is one of the spiritual aspects of my life that has changed. My prayer life was so bad that I attended every prayer seminar that came into the Houston area. I knew there had to be some secret to a deeper prayer life that I was missing, so I was determined to find it through learning about prayer. Whenever I tried to pray, my mind would wander and I would think about anything other than prayer—my work, what I would eat for lunch—anything except focused communication with my heavenly Father.

I had always resisted the discipline of writing my prayers. *It takes too long*, I rationalized. *Besides I talk faster than I can write, so it's more efficient.* Then in 1990, I began writing my prayers in a prayer journal. (A prayer journal is included in every First Place Member's Kit.) My prayer journal revolutionized my prayer life. When I prayed without writing the prayers, it was scattershot praying—"Lord, here comes Mary and she's got a bunch of problems. Help me know what to say." I never committed quality prayer time to the Lord.

When I write my prayers, I often don't know where to start, but I pick up my pen anyway and ask the Holy Spirit to help me pray. One morning I prayed for a friend of mine who led a group at another church. The Lord brought this friend into my mind and I prayed for her—without a particular reason.

When I got to work, I located her address and wrote her a brief card that told her "I prayed for you this morning." Before too long, the card came back and every blank space was covered with her writing. She told me about that particular day and how much she had needed and valued my prayers.

Jesus set the example of prayer for us. He taught His disciples to pray when He taught them the Lord's Prayer. Throughout Scripture we see that Jesus never relied on His own wisdom but on the Father's wisdom, because Jesus knew that He was living in a body of flesh on this earth. Look at an example in the book of Mark. Jesus had had an extremely busy day. He had healed many people, and I am quite sure He had gone to bed tired. But the Scripture tells us that "very early in the morning, while it was still dark, Jesus got up, left the house and went off to a solitary place, where he prayed" (Mark 1:35). We, too, must pray continually to have the power that we need to live this life.

In First Place, we learn to give God the first part of each day so that He can control our thoughts and actions for that day. During our quiet time, we learn to read our Bible. This is the time when God can speak to us through His Word. I have learned through the years that the Word of God must back up whatever I am thinking or whatever I am planning to do. The Bible must become the guidebook for every decision we make. We must become so acquainted with God's Word that we know the right way to think and the right way to act.

I believe our greatest example of how to live spiritually is our Lord, Jesus Christ. If Jesus needed to learn Scripture, then we should follow His example. The Bible tells us in Luke 2:46,47 that Jesus at age 12 had such a profound knowledge of the Scriptures that even the synagogue elders were amazed at His understanding. Jesus was the Son of God, but He was also as human as we are. He had to learn the Scriptures like we have to learn it. Only after we know God's Word and understand it can it make an impact on our lives. By memorizing Scripture, we have ready ammunition when tempted or when we need to minister to someone else. Just like the other areas of balance, this takes time. We must be patient and give God permission to change us, and He will.

EMOTIONAL

From everyone who has been given much, much will be demanded; and from the one who has been entrusted with much, much more will be asked (Luke 12:48).

The final area to bring into balance is our emotions. Each of us longs to attain balance in our emotional life. A few fortunate people have found emotional balance because they come from stable, loving families. If you are reading this book and the last sentence rings true for you, then you should celebrate the blessings of God in your life. It is rare to find any-one in our society who has emotional stability. Families are disintegrating at a rapid rate, and children are the victims of the breakup. A friend of mine, Dr. William Heston, says, "Not everybody came from dysfunctional homes, but everybody's home had some level of dysfunction. It's a matter of degrees."[1]

Many of us live totally out of our emotions. We eat because of our emotional state—if we are happy, we eat; if we are sad or depressed, we eat. Food is used to celebrate important occasions and eating becomes tied to our emotions. Many obese men and women have suffered from some form of abuse—physical, mental, emotional or sexual. At our First Place program at First Baptist Houston, we have offered First Place support courses. Through these courses participants learn about emotional healing. Only God can heal the emotional wounds of our past. Many of us have been taught that healing is instantaneous at the time of our salvation, so we should be able to forget about the emotional wounds from our past. This teaching is misleading because emotional healing is a process and is not instantaneous. Our salvation is the beginning of the process to become whole people emotionally. God longs to heal us of our emotional pain, and we are the only ones who can willingly give our pain to the Lord and permit our heavenly Father to deal with it. The act of surrender sounds simple and easy, but it takes a long time. Many survivors of abuse (whether sexual, emotional, physical or mental) use the illustration that the healing is like "God pulling back layer after layer as we can stand the pain." Our God is as gentle in the emotional area as He is in every other area of our lives. The pace of our emotional healing will never be faster than we choose. Still, God can't begin the process until we surrender our emotions into His capable hands.

I wish I could tell you that I have the emotional area of my life totally under control, but it's not true. Like you, my emotions ebb and flow. One week several years ago, when I was particularly down in the dumps, these negative feelings grew until I thought, *I can't even go into work. I can't smile or say anything, so I should stay home and regroup.* About 9:30 A.M. my husband was about to leave for work, and I had predetermined not to answer my telephone for the rest of the day.

As Johnny was walking out the door, the phone rang and he said, "Do you want me to answer it?"

I said, "Yes, please." When he learned who was on the phone, he told me the name. I thought it was a friend of mine (someone else), so I took the phone, and Johnny walked out the door. On the phone was a woman whom I had been lifting to the Lord in prayer for the last six months. I had asked God specifically to have her call me. I had told God, "I don't want to call her because You have all the power. If you want me to talk with her, then have her call me."

God has a great sense of humor because the woman called me on one of my lowest emotional days of the year. I had been crying and feeling sorry for myself about my awful day and then she called. I began to feel excited hearing her voice, and we talked for the next two hours. By the time I hung up the phone, my negative emotions had fled. God orchestrated that phone call, and then He gave me the emotional strength to handle the situation.

The Bible exhorts us to be prepared to talk about the Lord in season and out of season (see 2 Tim. 4:2). Personally, I'd rather talk with people in season than out of season. It used to be that almost every time I needed to give a speech, it came during my PMS time of the month. Everything during the day seemed black and horrible, yet in the midst of it all, God took me under His wings and gave me strength. His power is manifested through our weaknesses. I could have blocked out those days from my schedule and refused to teach, but I didn't. God could not heal me of this emotional situation until I was willing to make a positive step toward emotional healing. When I finally gave up caffeine, PMS became an emotional illness of my past, praise God!

In First Place, we believe that to give emotionally wounded people only a weight-loss plan is like putting a Band-Aid on a cancerous lesion. Many people have never succeeded in weight loss because they haven't dealt with their emotional pain. In First Place, weight loss is not our primary goal. You may participate in the program for a long time before you find success in weight loss, but I promise that during that time God will be working in other areas of your life. When we give the Lord first place in our life, He is the only one who knows what needs to transpire next. If you trust God with your emotions, then He will do the rest. Richard Chenevix Trench said, "None but God can satisfy the longing of the immortal soul; as the heart was made for Him, He only can fill it."[2] Within First Place, we constantly seek balance in life. We keep our four-sided balance symbol with each of the four aspects (mental, physical, spiritual and emotional) as a constant reminder about balance.

In the next chapter we begin to examine the details of the nine commitments in First Place. These commitments are the heart of the program, and I'm eager for you to begin. Let's continue the journey toward a Christ-centered life.

✳

THE FIRST SIX COMMITMENTS

Over the years, Carol J. White of Fort Walton Beach, Florida, tried almost every diet in existence. Her weight went up and down for years as she tried a fad diet that required fasting for one week, then a diet allowing only 1,000 calories the next, then fasting again. At one point, Carol took the drastic step of having her stomach stapled, which worked—for a while. She had given up on any attempts to keep weight off until a First Place group was started at her local church. The meeting was on the second floor and Carol's knees hurt with every step. She thought, *If I don't lose weight, I may not be able to walk in a few years—much less climb stairs.*

In August 1995, Carol, at age 59, began the First Place program. She weighed 267 pounds. The daily Bible study and Scripture reading along with morning prayer were a real inspiration for her. She says, "God gave me the strength and courage to face each day and convicted me that my eating habits were sinful and that I needed to change. I went sugar free the first session, and I can tell you that only God could do that with me."

Since her first session, Carol has lost 92 pounds and has led a couple of First Place groups. She emphasizes the importance of all aspects of the program: "My experience says you have to commit to all aspects if you are to succeed."

Commitment is an elusive quality in our world. It's almost impossible to get people to RSVP before an event. A more tragic example is evident in our families—at the first sign of relationship trouble, people drop their commitment to their spouse. The First Place program is built on nine commitments that, when followed, will draw you into a deeper relationship with Jesus Christ. In this chapter we will examine the first six commitments, which primarily relate to aspects of spiritual, mental and emotional health. In the next chapter, three more commitments, which are particularly related to aspects of physical health, will be explained.

These commitments are not listed in order of priority, or importance. Each element is essential in order for First Place to transform your life into one of balance. None of the commitments is difficult, but each is important to achieve balance. Let's examine each commitment and then determine if God wants you to become a part of this program called First Place.

COMMITMENT 1: ATTENDANCE

Though one may be overpowered, two can defend themselves.
A cord of three strands is not quickly broken (Eccles. 4:12).

Attendance at the First Place meeting is essential to success in the program. (We encourage you to seek a group in your area. See the ministry contact page in the back of the book for help with locating or starting a group.) When we miss a class, we suffer and the class suffers, because we need to meet together to gain mutual strength and encouragement. This commitment to attendance at the meetings means that we've made it a priority in our lives. We are committed not to let any other meetings or obligations take precedence over First Place. If for some reason someone cannot attend, then that person must call the class leader or someone else in the group. What would be a valid reason for not attending the meeting? Only the individual giving the reason knows if it is valid or not. (Someone once said that an excuse is a reason wrapped up in a lie.) A true reason for missing a meeting would be personal illness or the illness of a family member.

I once heard it said that 80 percent of life is showing up. This has proven to be true in my own life. I have to show up in every area of the First Place commitments. For example, in the area of exercise I can't remember a single morning when I woke up and said, "Oh, this is wonderful. I get to exercise today." On my own initiative—without any commitment—I would stay home, drink coffee and leisurely read my newspaper. But one of the commitments of First Place is exercise, and I know it's important. Therefore I get up and show up for exercise. Some days, as I take my first steps, I say to myself, *I'll only walk a mile*—but at least I'm doing something that 95 percent of the world doesn't do. I'm showing up. As I begin my morning walk, someone usually shows up at the track to walk with me. Invariably we begin talking and I end up walking farther than originally expected. I know that if I don't show up early on the track, then it's a cinch I won't work in exercise later. And when I do show up, I'm glad I've kept this commitment.

The commitment to attendance is like exercise. You have to show up. If you refuse, your day will not be any better—in fact, it may be worse. This commitment to attend the meetings was written into the First Place program from the beginning. This small group of people becomes your support group, helping you to grow in Christ and change your lifestyle. During the first couple of weeks the group bonds; therefore, after this time, new people must wait for a new session to start. This bonding is the glue that holds the group together. You will find that the individuals in your group form lasting friendships that extend far beyond the First Place class.

One of our groups at First Baptist Houston illustrates this deep bonding. After becoming a leader, one of our participants felt God's leading to emphasize a First Place group for women who weighed over 200 pounds. Because she had been in that position, she knew the hopeless feelings these women often feel, and she wanted to reach out to them. At the next orientation session to help people learn about First Place, this leader put a little asterisk on the commitment forms handed in by women in this weight category. Then she called each one of them and asked if they would be interested in this type of group. Each of them expressed enthusiasm for the idea.

At the first meeting, she recalls, "I had never seen so much hopelessness in a room. These women had a long way to go and a lot of weight to lose. They were skeptical about their possibilities for success." The leader wondered if such a specialized group was the right decision. During that first meeting, the group began to get acquainted and bond with each other. As the women succeeded on the First Place program, pounds were lost and their spirits lifted. After a few weeks, one of the women asked, "After we weigh under 200 pounds, does that mean we have to leave this group?"

The answer was no. The group stayed together. Their experience illustrates the deep level of friendship formed in a First Place group meeting.

Problems begin if we believe weight loss is the only reason to attend the meeting. If we have had a bad week and know we haven't lost any weight or maybe we've even gained weight, there is a tendency to not want to show up for the meeting. We hope our subsequent week will be better, and we can show a weight loss at the next meeting. We are deluded if we fall into this type of thinking, because attendance at the meeting is the only way to have a better week. Through our attendance, we receive emotional support from other people. It reaffirms that with God's help, we can do the entire program. When we attend even during a bad week, we learn to be transparent enough to ask for prayer in our struggles. Our fellow members will pray for us and then call or e-mail us during the next week to check on our progress. These phone calls and this encouragement from other people cannot happen unless we attend the meeting.

We also must believe that God is still working in our lives—even when we don't lose weight. The Lord knows the plans He has for us, and they are not cookie-cutter plans where each of us has exactly the same experience. God works in each life in His own way because each one of us has been created differently. Our responsibility is to simply be available to God for His use.

From the beginning, this attendance commitment should be easy to accomplish. We must determine in our minds that we need each other and that is the critical reason that we've joined the group. Remember,

success is in the process, not the program. If you don't quit, you will succeed.

What Happens During the Meeting?

Each First Place group meeting lasts 1 hour and 15 minutes. During the
first 15 minutes, everyone weighs in, and his or her weight is recorded.
People in the group say their memory verse for the week when they step
on the scales. The assistant collects the Commitment Records (see the
next chapter for a dicussion of this commitment) and weighs in each
member, leaving the leader free to chat with members while others are
weighing in and saying their memory verse. All weighing in is strictly
confidential and private.

Each meeting begins with prayer and then the leader guides the class
in a few minutes of sharing. During this portion of the meeting, the participants ask questions or discuss any problems they are having with any
aspect of First Place such as exercise, the Live-It plan or their plan for
encouragement of other members. Next, the leader guides the group in
a discussion of the Bible study for that particular week. During the final
portion of the meeting, the group shares prayer requests, and the meeting is closed in prayer. If time permits, the group stands in a circle and
hold hands, and members may pray if they so desire. Members don't
have to pray aloud unless they are comfortable praying in a group.

Why Should I Be Accountable?

Besides providing bonding, the First Place group holds each of us
accountable for the weight-loss goals and other goals we set at the beginning of the 13-week session. Accountability is a concept that Jesus
taught His disciples in Luke 17:3,4: "So watch yourselves. If your brother sins, rebuke him, and if he repents, forgive him. If he sins against you
seven times a day, and seven times comes back to you and says, 'I repent,'
forgive him." By joining and attending a First Place group, you are
accountable to your leader and the other members of your group. It's a
responsibility that you should begin with a solid understanding. You are
granting your leader permission to help you grow mentally, spiritually,
physically and emotionally.

Another reason for accountability is our presence in the Body of Christ. The apostle Paul uses the illustration of a physical body in 1 Corinthians 12:12-26. Verse 12 in this passage reads: "The body is a unit, though it is made up of many parts; and though all its parts are many, they form one body. So it is with Christ." Like a hand is physically connected to a body, the members of a First Place group are connected to each other.

When I lead a group, I am not a mean leader. In fact, some of the participants in my group have told me, "If you were a meaner leader, I'd do better in the program." I am not a diet cop, and I don't watch what people eat. Instead, my job is to encourage and motivate my group, so they leave the meeting uplifted and return having lost weight. God will provide the daily strength, but the individuals have to do the work of First Place. No one else can do it for them.

Some people refuse to be accountable to the group after they have joined. If that occurs, it means they may also have a problem with accountability to God. If they refuse to be accountable, then they don't weigh in, turn in a Commitment Record or learn the memory verse. Maybe they rebel by not sticking with the food plan and say, "I have to have my real Coke" or "I'm going to eat cake at the birthday party on Friday no matter what." If you are a leader and one of these individuals is in your group, don't take their rebellion personally. I have found that these people tend to refuse any sort of accountability.

Finally, accountability protects our freedom by limiting it. When you join a First Place class for 13 weeks, you agree to limit yourself to the nine commitments of the program. When I discipline myself to these commitments, I am continually amazed at how well the program works! When we live and work within the confines of God's laws, we have real freedom that the world can't begin to offer.

Can I Do the First Place Program on My Own?

It's important to address this common question. We have had people who are homebound follow the program, and they have had great success. For medical reasons, these people simply could not attend a class. (Others may be unable to locate a group nearby and may choose to begin

First Place on their own.) God honors their willingness to follow the commitments on their own, and they have succeeded in the program. Yet even in these situations, they still needed to call a friend and discuss their struggles and/or progress.

I personally believe there is great power in the group. A group doesn't have to be large—maybe at first it is only two or three people. As we discussed before, the group brings accountability; and without the accountability of a weekly meeting, most of us would never truly get started. (First Place offers a leader's guide and video for those who would like to do the program.) God has designed our lives for accountability. We know our bank expects us to have money in our account before we write a check. We understand that unless we come to work each day, we won't receive our paycheck. If we understand this aspect of accountability, why is it difficult to understand that accountability is the key for balance in every area of life? When you commit to attend a First Place meeting, you have taken the first step.

COMMITMENT 2: ENCOURAGEMENT

A friend loves at all times (Prov. 17:17).

The second commitment in First Place is to contact each week one person in your group or an accountable friend if you are not in a group. The most important reason for the contact is to reach out to others and encourage them. How you contact them—whether in person or by another means—doesn't matter. What's essential is that we honor and support each other, building on our common problems and goals. When we begin First Place, we've already admitted that we have one problem in common—we need to learn to eat properly. And most of us probably also have a need to start exercising and setting aside time for Bible study and prayer. Awareness of this common bond makes it easier to reach out to other members in the group and give them encouragement.

Why Should I Encourage Others?

From my years in the church, even in Sunday School, I've found that people find it difficult to talk with others about their problems. We need to move beyond the superficial sort of communication that occurs in the hallway of a church.

As a member of a First Place group, we can be involved in each other's lives and take the time to care about another person. A simple phone call, e-mail, card or personal visit during the week can make an enormous difference in another person's routine. To this individual, it points out that this group is different. Within the confines of First Place, you can feel that someone cares enough to listen to your sorrows and joys. We want to be here for you.

Some people are afraid of making that first contact; however, most have found that this encouragement commitment marks the beginning of a new opportunity and ministry. We need to recognize the importance of keeping this weekly encouragement commitment. It amounts to one tiny step in love to reach out to others who need it.

Why Is Reaching Out Hard for Me?

Most First Place participants find encouraging others hard to do. Perhaps it is because we have been rejected and hurt many times in the past. We may have built walls around ourselves to keep people from ever hurting us again. I believe that God wants to begin emotional healing in each First Place participant.

Through my experience in First Place I have learned how to truly love other people, some of whom the world had already given a strong message that they would never amount to anything or be useful. Yet God tells us something quite different. He says He loves every individual as much as He loves you and me. Whatever the individuals have done or whatever sins they have committed doesn't matter.

God's Word teaches that there are no degrees of sin; one sin is not more horrible than another. God says all sin separates us from Him. That's why it's important that we not only confess our sin to Him, but we also must reach out in love to those around us; then we can forgive those who have committed sin against us.

This process of reaching out in love to others takes time. You will not be able to do it overnight, but God will empower you to forgive those who have sinned against you. When we refuse to forgive someone, it's as if that person were sitting in a chair strapped to our back, and we carry them around all our lives. Our unforgiveness doesn't hurt the other person, but it hurts us tremendously.

The root problem here is love. Perhaps we've never felt truly loved or able to love others. When the teachers of the Law asked Jesus to identify the greatest commandment, He said to them, "'Love the Lord your God with all your heart and with all your soul and with all your mind and with all your strength.' The second is this: 'Love your neighbor as yourself.' There is no commandment greater than these" (Mark 12:30,31). This command is repeated in three of the Gospels. If Jesus said that it was the greatest commandment, then He meant it.

Many of us have a problem accepting and showing love. Maybe as children we didn't receive enough love; or we didn't receive unconditional love from our parents, teachers or other significant people in our lives. As a result, loving ourselves, as well as God, may be difficult. We may find God's unconditional love, as described throughout Scripture, difficult to comprehend. Therefore, reaching out and loving others is difficult for us. Yet when we are filled with God's love, we are able to love others (see 1 John 4:21).

As we continue in the First Place program, we learn that God loves us just the way we are—warts and all. God doesn't leave us on our own, but as we turn our hearts and daily lives over to His capable hands, He is committed to conforming us to the image of His Son, Jesus. If you find it difficult to reach out to others because of being hurt in the past, then you need to pray and ask God to show you one person in your group whom you can trust. Ask God to help you bond with one person that you can reach out to and who will love you back. God will honor your prayers and begin to teach you about His love. As He demonstrates His love through others, He's going to give you the courage to trust and love in return.

What Do I Say?
When you make that first contact with another First Place member, you already know you have a common bond. You can always begin the conver-

sation or correspondence with a typical First Place question, "How is your week going?" The person with whom you make contact may be experiencing a good week; then you can celebrate together. If not, don't feel responsible for fixing the problems or making his or her week a success. Just listening and caring will mean a great deal to the other person. If you have a suggestion to share, share it in a manner that leaves the person free to accept it or not.

Your e-mail, phone call, card or in-person contact enables you to be aware of what's going on in someone else's life. This type of detailed conversation will not always happen on the first contact, yet it occurs as you cultivate trust and friendship. Often we feel that our food temptations are greater than anyone else's, or we may feel that our life experiences are such that no one would understand them—each of us thinks, *I am the only one who has been through this*. Yet personal contact assures us that other people have suffered like we have and they struggle in the same areas. We discover that God has healed others and wants to heal us, too. As we are healed, we can become part of the process for healing in others.

Many people relate that they had a cookie or a piece of cake in their hand when someone called from their group. Some put the caller on hold while they disposed of the cookie. The Holy Spirit urged that call at the perfect time. Many times when you call, you'll hear, "I am so glad you called. You don't know what I'm going through right now." Or someone will call you when you are having a particularly difficult day.

Pray for the person before you contact him or her. If you make a phone call or a personal visit, don't neglect to pray together and praise God for working through both of you. Add a Scripture or prayer if you send a card or e-mail. A few years ago I learned from a friend in Atlanta to cultivate the habit of telephone prayer. Whenever I talk with her, she says, "Well, let's pray together." It has become such a blessing to me to pray over the phone with fellow Christians.

I hope that you will incorporate prayer into your encouragement commitment—no matter what means you choose to use. If you are with the person or on the phone with them, you can say, "Could we pray together before we say good-bye?" Ask God to bless that person and wrap His arms around them that day. Allow the other person to pray for you before you finish the visit. I am always uplifted when I hear someone taking my name to God's throne of grace.

Prayer is now such an important part of my life that I never start a meeting without it. Nor do I conduct a counseling situation without praying together at the start and end of the session. God blesses our lives when we ask Him—and He wants His children to come to Him and ask Him! So don't neglect praying with the people in your group. Then praise God after the meeting is over for the things He has accomplished during your time together.

How Am I Helped by Encouragement?

I believe God wants to use men and women who have suffered terribly and have begun to heal to minister to others. I believe God was there when they were enduring such pain. He loves them so much that He will not only heal but also use them in the very same area where they have suffered.

I see men and women today who have been healed or who are being healed of some form of abuse, reaching out to other men and women who have been abused and loving them through Christ. I see people who are struggling with a health condition being strengthened by others with the same condition.

You might not realize it now, but encouraging others is a wonderful way to receive encouragement. You can take heart in knowing that someone else experiences your temptations, your failures. You can have hope for yourself when you see that someone else has overcome those temptations, has turned failures into success. Encouragement is a twofold blessing: it blesses the one giving and the one receiving.

So don't be afraid to reach out to others. See in them struggles that you share. See in them the joy and the peace that living out First Place can bring. Encourage them—and you will be encouraged!

COMMITMENT 3: PRAYER

If you remain in me and my words remain in you, ask whatever you wish, and it will be given you (John 15:7).

Personal Prayer Time

Your commitment to prayer is one of the most important commitments in the First Place program. When I began First Place, I didn't have much of a prayer life. I could do almost everything else but pray. When it came to talking on the phone for an hour, I didn't have a problem. At my work, I could concentrate for long periods of time. When I started to pray, however, I was easily distracted and began to think about my breakfast plans or what I would accomplish when I got to work. My mind wandered so much that after a few days of trying, I gave up praying at the beginning of my day.

Instead, I prayed with "shoot-up" prayers. If I didn't spend time alone with God, then I shot up prayers during my day when I had a need. When I was first involved in First Place, I was not yet the national director. My work involved supervising the various secretaries in the Education Department of First Baptist Houston. One of the women I supervised was continually late to work. When she did arrive, she headed to the bathroom to put on her makeup. This girl and I did not get along; and early one morning as I was exercising, I shot up a prayer, "Lord, how can I get her fired?"

In a still, small voice the Lord said, "Carole, I love her as much as I love you."

I could not believe this response. "Lord, this can't be. She's obnoxious." Yet I began to pray that God would love her through me because I sure couldn't do it on my own. That day when I got to work, I knew where to find her—in the bathroom. I walked in and said, "I need to talk with you." She looked at me expectantly. I continued, "If I have ever done anything to hurt you, I want to ask for your forgiveness."

Tears welled up in her eyes, and she said, "Oh, Carole, I thought you hated me."

I told her honestly, "No, I want to help you be successful here." From that moment on, we became friends. Changing the way I prayed changed me and my attitude toward her. I learned that when I don't love someone, God can love that person through me until I begin to truly love him or her myself.

Shoot-up praying works in a pinch, but our heavenly Father wants a personal relationship with His children, and relationships take time. To have that intimate relationship, we must spend time daily in prayer with God. When you join the First Place program, determine what time of day is best for you to have a quiet time alone with God. Morning is my best time of the day. I wake up alert, and early in the day I can give my best to God. Your life may be different. Perhaps you have small children at home and no matter how much you try, you cannot get up in the morning before your children. If you identify with this situation, nap time might be your best time of day for a quiet time with God. If you work outside the home, maybe you can arrive to work early and have your quiet time at your desk. If you live alone, maybe you prefer to have your quiet time in the evening. Because of family obligations, evening is the most difficult time for most people. Whatever time you select, it needs to be when you can be alone. The quiet time for prayer loses its meaning with frequent interruptions.

There are several reasons why the First Place program encourages you to write your prayers during your quiet time. First, when you write, your mind can't wander. If my mind starts to wander, my pen stops and I am immediately reminded to continue praying. A second reason for writing prayers is to provide a written record of what God is doing in your life. I love to go back through my journal and highlight the prayers God has answered.

One morning during my time of prayer, I felt led to pray for one of our leaders in another church. When I got to work that morning, I sent her a note and told her that I had prayed for her. About a week later I received a note that read, "You will never know what it meant to me to know that you were praying for me that day. It was a witness to my spirit that the Holy Spirit impressed you to pray." Then in the letter, she told me about various events in her life and how much turmoil filled every day. The Holy Spirit has the power to unite believers through the power of prayer. Through your regular use of a prayer journal, you can tap into that power source.

A third reason to write our prayers is to learn the natural progression for prayer. In First Place, we use the ACTS method of praying.

If you write ACTS in an acrostic, it looks like this:

A   Adoration

C   Confession

T   Thanksgiving

S   Supplication

A—Adoration. When you begin your time of prayer, start by adoring God for His character and for everything He has done in your life. For your first attempt, you might find this awkward; but with a little practice you will find that adoring, or praising, God will elevate your mind to the right attitude for prayer. Sometimes I get a songbook and read the words from a song to God. Other days, I sing a praise chorus to the Lord. You might enjoy reading a psalm to God. The goal is to establish an attitude of worship in your quiet time.

C—Confession. After you have established an attitude of praise, allow your heart to look inward. If you sit quietly, the Holy Spirit will bring into your mind anything that you need to confess to God. If you are a beginner in prayer, at first you might have to write down a long list things to confess and ask God to forgive each one. After you confess these areas to God, tear up the list as a physical symbol that God has forgiven each one. Now you are clean to go before Him in prayer. After this initial time of cleansing, you will find that sin doesn't accumulate if you go to the Father each day.

Confession and repentance go hand in hand. The Bible says in 1 John 1:9, "If we confess our sins, he is faithful and just and will forgive us our sins and purify us from all unrighteousness." When we sincerely confess our sin to God (which means we are sorry), then we ask God to forgive and to remove the sin from our lives. If we confess the same sin each day, then we haven't repented and are simply telling God about our awareness of the sin. Confession is one of the hard areas in prayer. We like to make excuses for our sins. For example, we tell God and other people, "That's just the way I am." Oftentimes, we justify our own sins, yet we are quick to point out the sins in others. Through true confession we come into a right relationship with God and move into thanksgiving and petition.

T—Thanksgiving. Philippians 4:6,7 says: "Do not be anxious about anything, but in everything, by prayer and petition, with thanksgiving, present your requests to God. And the peace of God, which transcends all understanding, will guard your hearts and your minds in Christ Jesus." When we begin to thank God for the many blessings of life, a peace fills our minds and hearts. We may think things look pretty bleak; but as we thank God for our health, our family, a home with electric lights and running water, then life comes into perspective. Henry Blackaby, the author of *Experiencing God*, wrote about the necessity of returning to our spiritual markers when we pray. These spiritual markers are times from our past when God did a mighty work in our lives. When we thank God for our spiritual markers, it returns us to a place where our lives are once again in clear focus. God wants our focus removed from ourselves and turned to Him. Our thanksgiving will accomplish this shift of focus.

S—Supplication. In our time of supplication, we ask God for anything that we need. For many of us, our entire prayer lives have centered on this portion of prayer. When prayers are limited to asking God for needs, then they become a grocery list, telling God what He needs to do for us.

A few years ago I discovered Isaiah 65:24, which says, "Before they call I will answer; while they are still speaking I will hear." This Scripture has burned into my heart and soul; it has taught me that God knows my every need before I even ask. Yet even though God knows my needs in advance, I still need to ask. As another Scripture says, "If you, then, though you are evil, know how to give good gifts to your children, how much more will your Father in heaven give good gifts to those who ask him!" (Matt. 7:11). Our heavenly Father is more loving than our finite minds can imagine. If you are a parent and your child makes a request, you will move heaven and Earth to meet that request. There are many things that we would love to do, if our children would only ask. During the Christmas season I have seen parents go to 10 different stores to locate something their child has requested. We love our children, and our heavenly Father loves us. He wants to give us the desires of our hearts if we will give Him first place in everything.

Corporate Prayer

A second facet of prayer in First Place is the prayer time at each First Place meeting. We believe in the importance of prayer, so we pray at the beginning and at the end of every meeting. Usually the time of prayer to conclude each meeting lasts about 15 minutes. During this time, participants ask for prayer for themselves or for needs that affect their success in the program. We encourage people to limit prayer requests to personal needs. As you make yourself vulnerable enough to ask for prayer for your specific needs, you will see the mighty power of prayer at work. One lady in my 6:15 A.M. class was having severe marital problems. Sometimes she barely got inside the door before she burst into tears. To attend the meeting, she had a long drive early in the morning. She would literally hold her tears in until she arrived at the meeting. Our group surrounded her and prayed with her, so she could face the day. As a First Place group, we rallied around this hurting person.

Another element we emphasize with corporate prayer is that prayer requests stay inside the group. We ask each participant to never share a prayer request with anyone outside the group. As a result, the members of the group know their requests will remain confidential. From my experience, members honor this request and place the prayer needs into God's capable hands for His answer. When we have a safe place for our requests, we can voice the request and it ceases to have power over us. It has been said that we are only as sick as our secrets. God never intended for the Christian life to be private. Personal, yes, but not private. Most of us have never been part of a group where we could be transparent and vulnerable, even at our own church. First Place groups are different because through joining the group, you have already admitted you have one problem in common. Either you need to lose some weight or you have admitted that you want a closer relationship with God. The group environment fosters honesty. Please don't misunderstand me; these groups are not a time for a pity party. The weekly meetings are extremely positive, but there is always time to stop and pray for a hurting member. Prayer is the underpinning for the Body of Christ.

COMMITMENT 4: BIBLE READING

Your word is a lamp to my feet and a light for my path (Ps. 119:105).

I am very grateful for Christian parents who took me to church and taught me God's Word. In church, we memorized Bible verses and were taught to read and study God's Word for direction in life. This may not be your story.

You might join a First Place group and not own a Bible, or you might have to dust off an old one and take it to the meeting. Many leaders have purchased Bibles for group members because they did not own one. While on the surface our nation professes to be Christian, many people grow up with no idea what the Bible says or how to apply it personally to their lives. While writing this book, I have been reminded of the enduring truth of God's Word in my life. God will bring a Scripture passage to my mind and insert it into the text. If I don't recall where it is located in the Bible, I can find the reference through my Bible concordance. This type of experience will be foreign to you if you have no working knowledge of the Bible. God cannot put something in your mind that is not already there.

When you are seeking consolation and help, the Bible will become a familiar companion that will speak God's word to you in times of trouble. As you read the Bible on a consistent and regular basis, your personal relationship with your heavenly Father becomes deeper, more meaningful. Prayer is speaking to God, but Scripture reading is God speaking to us. It is probably more important that God speak to us than that we speak to God. After I finish my prayer time, I read my Bible because I am more in the frame of mind to listen to God.

The First Place Member's Guide includes a systematic Bible reading plan, so you can read the entire Bible in a one-year period. You just look up the particular reading for each day. You can also use a one-year Bible, which is available in several different Bible translations. With a one-year Bible, the Scripture passages are divided each day into a selection from the Old Testament, the New Testament, psalms and proverbs. I use a one-year Bible because it's easy to use and I read more using this system.

This commitment to read Scripture doesn't depend on how much or how little you read each day. Instead, it is important to ask God to give you insight from the Bible that will help you in the activities of today. Sometimes after reading one chapter, or even a few verses, the Holy Spirit might direct you to stop on a particular verse. After you read that verse a few times, God may give you some insight into a current problem. Through that particular verse from His Word, God can speak to you. The Bible says, "All Scripture is God-breathed and is useful for teaching, rebuking, correcting and training in righteousness, so that the man of God may be thoroughly equipped for every good work" (2 Tim. 3:16,17).

Our goal in Scripture reading is to develop a systematic plan of reading. If you are unfamiliar with the Bible, you might begin with the Gospel of John. Read this Gospel several times until you understand what it says; then continue with another book of the Bible. There is no right or wrong way to read God's Word. The goal of this commitment is for participants to read their Bibles as a regular way of life. As you meet the commitment of Scripture reading, we hope God will give you a love for His Word that will last throughout your life.

COMMITMENT 5: SCRIPTURE MEMORY VERSE

I have hidden your word in my heart that I might not sin against you (Ps. 119:11).

Each 13-week First Place session includes 10 weeks of Bible study. Each week a memory verse is selected that relates to the study. During the week, participants commit to memorize this verse and to recite it when they weigh in on a scale at the weekly meeting. The memory verse commitment isn't a difficult one. If you participate in First Place for a full year, you will be able to memorize 40 Bible verses. Scripture memory is important because these verses become valuable tools God can use when we face temptation or problems. He also uses these verses so that we can help other people who are struggling and need our encouragement.

Once a preacher told his congregation, "Whenever you have a problem, you should ask God for a verse of Scripture to help you." The next Sunday a woman confronted the preacher and said, "Your advice about asking God for a Bible verse doesn't work for me." Then she went on to explain, "Three times last week I had a difficulty, so I asked God for a Scripture and nothing happened." The wise preacher smiled and said, "Of the three verses you have memorized, maybe none of them applied." For some of us, this story is all too true. Possibly the only verse you have memorized is John 3:16. Or maybe you have never memorized a single verse from the Bible. I have good news for you—it is never too late to start memorizing God's Word.

One summer I heard T. W. Hunt speak. He is the author of many books, including two of my favorites: *Disciple's Prayer Life* and *The Mind of Christ*. To my surprise, Dr. Hunt said that even though he is past retirement age, he continues to memorize Scripture. He admitted, "Scripture memory has always been difficult for me, but I continue memorizing the Bible in spite of it." Then Dr. Hunt described memorizing entire chapters from the Bible. He memorizes these chapters also as separate verses, so he can quote any verse in the chapter apart from the whole. As a child, I memorized whole chapters of the Bible, but I am not able to isolate a single verse in the chapter and say it. Dr. Hunt has accomplished quite a feat—especially for someone with difficulty memorizing Scripture. He also mentioned that he practices his memory work on his grandchildren. What a legacy Dr. Hunt is leaving to them! They will never forget the importance of Scripture memory in the life of their grandfather.

If you feel that you cannot possibly memorize the verse for the week, then write the verse five times each day and turn it in at your meeting. After writing the Bible verse, many people tell us they have memorized it. During your time in First Place, you should consider Scripture memorization as a gift to yourself.

Several years ago Martha Norsworthy, a First Place leader in Murray, Kentucky, told me how the Scripture memory commitment ministered to her during a desperate crisis in her life. Two days before Christmas, Martha's only daughter, Carol, and son-in-law, Bryan, were killed while driving the church van to deliver Christmas presents to the children of their mission families. A woman who was drunk drove her car through an intersection and hit the couple. The van burst into flames and the couple died.

At the time of the crash, Martha was leading a First Place group. When Martha arrived at the crash site, she knew there was no use hoping someone survived. Immediately the Lord brought to her mind and heart that week's memory verse—Hebrews 12:1, "Therefore, since we are surrounded by such a great cloud of witnesses, let us throw off everything that hinders and the sin that so easily entangles, and let us run with perseverance the race marked out for us." For Martha, this verse became like a huge billboard especially for her. Suddenly she understood that Carol and Bryan were in that great cloud of witnesses and that God had a race marked out for her. Martha's First Place group became her support group as she went through the grieving process. When this tragedy struck, Martha had already lost 80 pounds. During her time of mourning, she went on maintenance without gaining back any of her weight. (Many of you understand the victory in this part of the story. As overeaters from emotional reasons, we surely would regain every lost pound in a tragedy of this magnitude—if we didn't have God's help.)

First Place members and leaders are not exempt from problems, but we know our strength comes only from the Lord. Christians do not grieve as the world grieves, because we know the end-of-the-world story has already been written. If our loved ones know Christ, one day we will surely see them again in heaven. Martha said Carol and Bryan had been in First Place and that two of the precious items left behind were their prayer journals. On the pages of these journals, they wrote about the numerous changes God was making in their spiritual growth. These journals provided written reassurance for Martha that they were ready to meet God, even if she wasn't ready to give them up.

As you begin First Place, you will be amazed at how God uses this commitment to memorize Scripture in your own life. Whatever you do for God is never wasted. God knows everything that you face today, as well as the things you will face in the future. The Lord will use your obedience in Scripture memory to equip you for anything that lies ahead.

With the Scripture memory songs developed by Rick Crawford and Jeff Nelson, you have an excellent resource to help you memorize your verse each week. The 10 memory verses from each Bible study have been set to music with an exercise tempo and placed on a CD which is included as a part of each Bible study. (Audiocassettes of these verses are also available.) Play these CDs in your car while running errands, at home while doing chores, at work during your breaks or while exercising. Each CD starts with a song to warm up, gradually speeds up to songs with an aerobic intensity and has a cooldown song at the end. Each song is written with the Scripture reference at the beginning. Then the song is presented in sections to help you memorize small segments at a time. Before the song ends, the entire verse is repeated. An interlude of music before the next Scripture verse gives you an opportunity to say the verse once more to yourself.

The following guidelines will also help make Scripture memorization easier. If you put these into practice, I believe Scripture memorization will become one of the joys of your life.

1. Always state where the Scripture passage is found. Much of the Scripture that I memorized as a child lacks an address in my mind. Consequently, when a Scripture comes into my thoughts, I must locate it in a concordance. If you develop the habit of always quoting the book, chapter and verse along with the Scripture, you will never have this predicament.

2. Scripture is hard to remember when it is just words without pictures. Anything that has a picture attached will stick in your memory. I remember once when my granddaughter Cara, who was in second grade at the time, was struggling with her spelling. On Monday evenings she would come to our home, and we would make a game of learning her words. She recalled learning the word "spaghetti" because of the silly way I taught her to remember it. I told her to imagine a lady named Hetti with spaghetti on her head. Whenever she had to spell spaghetti, she would think of spag-Hetti! In the same manner, you can

do this to memorize verses from the Bible: just take the verse apart and insert pictures for words that are hard to remember. For example, if you were memorizing Romans 15:13, you might think of your two teenagers, 15 and 13, who are always "roaming" around.

3. After memorizing a verse, try to quote it when talking with someone. After you use the verse a few times in conversation, the verse will be more firmly planted in your mind. You need to repeatedly use a Bible verse to incorporate that verse into your life.

4. If you and your family memorize Scripture together, then when your children become teenagers, your job as a parent will be much easier. Psalm 119:11 says, "I have hidden your word in my heart that I might not sin against you." If you encourage your family to memorize God's Word, then this key information and insight will be in their minds and hearts to instruct them. Then when your children are troubled or have problems with peer pressure, you can remind them of a memorized Scripture verse. Better still, some of the teens that I know can quote Scripture to their parents when they are discouraged. God's Word will bond a family together in a magnificent way.

Through the First Place Bible studies we also learn to pray Scripture. The last two days of each Bible study teach participants how to pray Scripture. As we learn to pray back to God the memory verses we learn, the verses become deeply rooted in our lives.

COMMITMENT 6: BIBLE STUDY

Do your best to present yourself to God as one approved, a workman who does not need to be ashamed and who correctly handles the word of truth (2 Tim. 2:15).

This commitment to Bible study is closely linked with Scripture reading. The distinction is that in addition to reading from the Bible, we study a specific area for the entire week and we use discussion questions. The commitment isn't overwhelming because within the First Place program, we answer only a few questions each day. It only takes 10 minutes or so. During the course of the week, we gain insight into God's Word for us. Then when the group comes together for our First Place meeting (or with your smaller accountability group of friends if you are not in a First Place meeting), we discuss the Bible study and what it meant to each of us that week. First Place has eight different 10-week Bible studies. Each week has five days of questions related to the Scriptures we are studying. Then days six and seven are for reflection on the memory verse, as well as learning tips on how both to memorize Scripture and to use Scripture as a basis for your prayers. With eight Bible studies, you could participate in the First Place program for two years without repeating a single study.

And yet I love to repeat the First Place Bible studies. When I repeat a study, I am at a point in my spiritual journey different from where I was the last time. It is incredible to me how the Bible, which was written thousands of years ago, is always relevant to my situation today. The exact same verses will speak to me in a different way according to my current need. The Bible itself describes Scripture: "The word of God is living and active. Sharper than any double-edged sword, it penetrates even to dividing soul and spirit, joints and marrow; it judges the thoughts and attitudes of the heart" (Heb. 4:12).

Another means to dig deeper into Bible study is with some additional resources outside of the First Place study. The following resources will enhance your study time in God's Word. To spread out the expense, you may want to acquire these various books over a period of time.

1. *Different translations.* Choose a Bible translation that speaks to you. Some of us grew up hearing the *King James Version*, and it is familiar. There are many excellent modern translations such as the *New International Version*, the *New Century Version*, the *New Living Translation* or the *New American Standard*. Spend a few minutes in a local Christian bookstore and try out some familiar passages in different versions; then select the one that

speaks to your heart. Each First Place Bible study is written for use with the *New International Version*. Using any other version while working on your Bible study may make answering the questions more difficult.

2. *Parallel Bible.* This type of Bible includes two to four translations. When we study God's Word, it is often useful to read several different translations because each one gives a different insight into the verse.

3. *An unabridged concordance.* This book contains an alphabetized listing of the words from the Bible. A concordance will help you to study different topics or words from the Bible.

4. *A Bible commentary.* In a commentary, the author explains the Bible passage and some of the scholarly background. These commentaries will give you a broader understanding of the Bible passage. There are a wide variety of commentaries available, either in a single volume for the entire Bible or in multiple volumes.

5. *A Bible dictionary.* This reference tool will give you insight into the cultural background of the Bible and help you understand definitions of difficult Bible terms like "atonement" and "sanctification."

As an alternative to several of these resources, consider buying a good study Bible. Like the variety of translations, there are many different study Bibles available. Again, visit your local Christian bookstore and look through the various Bible types. Talk with the salespeople to make an informed decision.

As you begin to dig deep and study God's Word, many new insights about God will jump from the pages into your mind and heart.

With these first six commitments, we've covered many components of the First Place program. I hope you are beginning to see that these commitments are little bite-sized pieces that anyone can accomplish in a short amount of time. In particular, commitments three through six are the spiritual commitments—those which Christians should be doing already. From our experience at First Place, many Christians are not embracing and fulfilling these commitments on a regular basis. Because these believers lack accountability in their lives, many days and months pass without any planned growth in the spiritual area. First Place offers an opportunity for gaining discipline in these spiritual areas of life, for those Christians in whom it may be lacking.

We've explained six of the nine commitments thus far. You've been faithful in our journey together through the First Place program. In the next chapter, we move into the physical part of our program and the food exchanges. Turn the page and let's continue our journey to a Christ-centered life.

*

CHAPTER SEVEN

THE FINAL THREE COMMITMENTS

For David Holmes, involvement with the First Place program was not a group experience. Over the years, David's weight had climbed until he weighed 300 pounds. In February 1995, David was the minister of music at a church in Nesbit, Mississippi. He felt the need to lose weight, so one Saturday night David joined Weight Watchers and attended a meeting. The next day his wife, Melanie, saw an ad for First Place in a Baptist publication. The couple then located First Place materials in a bookstore. David began the program and committed himself to the nine commitments. His accountability came from a couple of close friends and his wife, Melanie.

Like many people, David initially entered the plan for weight loss. His weight dropped to 192 pounds, but from his perspective the program exploded his spiritual life. "I had not consistently had a quiet time with the Lord before I started the First Place program," David says. Even while on the staff of a church, David had not consistently met alone with the Lord until he started the nine commitments.

After completing the first 13-week study on his own, David attracted some attention from others in his congregation. They asked him to lead a First Place group. He led a group through the first level of Bible studies, while on his own he completed the second level. For the next session, David led the group through the second study as he was completing the third one. David and his family are now in Decatur, Alabama, where David serves as the minister of music for his church. David has led several First Place classes in his church in Alabama but says that he tries to stay on the First Place program whether or not he is leading a class. "Initially I started for weight loss and that came, but the greatest benefit from the program was how my spiritual life was strengthened from First Place."

In this chapter we will look at the last three commitments of the First Place program. These three commitments predominately emphasize the physical aspects of a balanced life.

Because the majority of this chapter will focus on the physical aspects of First Place, it is valuable to spend a few moments looking at how to change our habits. Good and bad habits are formed through repetition, and eating habits are no exception. If you snack in front of the television, it's because you did it once. And the next time you reached for a snack while watching TV reinforced the habit. You kept repeating the behavior until it became a part of you. Some other habits include eating while reading, eating the minute you come in the house, eating when the kids come in from school, eating when you come in from a date and eating while cooking dinner.

We also eat when certain moods and circumstances come into our life—even when we are not hungry. Anger, boredom, fatigue, happiness, loneliness, nervousness, anxiety, the kids are finally in bed, our spouse is out for the evening or out of town, our spouse brings home candy or ice cream—all of these may trigger an eating response. Our goal in First Place is not only to break these old habits but also to form new ones through repetition. As you meet the commitments each day, you form good habits.

It is difficult to resist temptation; however, if you succeed in resisting the first time, then it becomes easier the next occasion. Before long, you have formed a good habit of resisting temptation. If you yield to temptation, you will find it easier to yield the next time.

Here are nine suggestions for new habits that you should develop. They will change your behavior if you consistently repeat them and they become a part of your life.

1. *Eat three meals a day.* Have two or three planned snacks daily.

2. *Prolong your meals* by eating slowly, putting down your eating utensil between each bite and not picking it up again until you have swallowed the bite, and hesitating between bites.

3. *Choose a specific place in your home or office to eat* all of your meals. This will become your designated eating place and should not be changed. Eating at your desk at work will make you prone to eat all day long, not just during mealtime. Eat in the lunchroom, cafeteria or designated eating area when you're at work.

4. *Make your designated eating place as attractive as possible.* At home, use good dishes, glasses and silverware. Add a place mat and napkin to complete the setting. Making your table setting attractive makes the food you are eating more pleasing. Even if you are eating alone at home, an attractive table makes your dining more enjoyable.

5. *When eating, avoid other activities* such as reading, watching TV, talking on the phone or working. When eating out, focus on what is going on around you. Enjoy your meal with friends or coworkers. If at home alone, focus on what you plan to do that morning, afternoon or evening. Clean up the dishes as soon as you have finished eating.

6. *Keep food only in the kitchen,* with tempting foods such as cookies and chips out of sight in a pantry or cabinet. Store items in opaque containers, so you won't see what is in them. Out of sight—out of mind.

7. *Avoid buying junk food,* even when you feel strapped for time, since no one in your family benefits from it.

8. *When possible, serve individual plates* from the stove rather than family style on the table. When you are unable to do this, put the serving dishes on the end opposite from where you are sitting.

9. *Serve yourself on a smaller plate.*

10. *Develop a habit of leaving at least one bite of each item* on your plate. If you can master this, it becomes easier to stop eating when you feel full. You will be used to leaving food on your plate.

Each of these 10 suggestions relates to eating habits. Substitute another activity for your old eating habits. Some substitute suggestions include taking a walk; enjoying a long bath; calling a friend; getting out of the house; writing a letter; reading a book; completing your Bible study; practicing your memory verse; reading your Bible; and taking up a hobby such as cross-stitch, painting, floral arrangement, ceramics, woodworking, gardening, genealogical research or sports.

COMMITMENT 7: LIVE-IT

Do you not know that your body is a temple of the Holy Spirit, who is in you, whom you have received from God? You are not your own; you were bought at a price. Therefore honor God with your body (1 Cor. 6:19,20).

"Live-It" is the First Place word for diet. The word "diet" is too morbid sounding for a Christian. The first three letters spell "die." Life is meant for living, and the Christian's life—with Christ in first place—is meant to be lived abundantly. So let's "live-it," not "die-it."

Our Live-It plan is based on the USDA Food Pyramid and involves a food exchange system to help you develop well-balanced eating habits. First Place uses the same terminology as the American Diabetic Association, the American Dietetic Association and the American Heart Association; therefore, a portion of food is known as an exchange. The food plan is divided into six food groups:

1. Bread/Starch
2. Vegetable
3. Fruit
4. Meat
5. Milk
6. Fat

A well-balanced meal includes food from each of these groups. Many people believe that it doesn't really matter what they eat as long as they aren't fat. But I know many thin people who are in extremely poor health. In his book *Nutrition for God's Temple*, Dr. Dick Couey has remarked:

> Sins against the body are costly. Our bodies deteriorate from heart disease, high blood pressure, diabetes, and cancer, which in many instances can be prevented by proper diet and exercise. You can neglect your body's physical needs, which often leads to poor health, or glorify God in your body, which often leads to good health. Your witness to the world and your well-being depend on the choices you make.[1]

A key part of the Live-It plan is education. This section will help you understand some key factors about food consumption. First, there are approximately 45 known nutrients our bodies need each day. These nutrients are grouped into six classes: water, carbohydrates, lipids, proteins, vitamins and minerals. Unless we get these nutrients in the required amounts, our bodies cannot build strong healthy cells. Most of us don't know which nutrients are in which foods, so the exchange system has been developed as an easy way to choose good nutrition. Each food group includes a wide variety of food selections, and we know that each choice in a particular food group has basically the same nutritional makeup.

Here are some basic recommendations for the Live-It plan:

- Whenever possible, eat fresh fruits and vegetables instead of canned or frozen ones.
- Use whole-grain wheat products rather than white-flour or refined products.
- Eliminate high-fat cheeses when possible.
- Bake and broil meats, and eat large quantities of fish and chicken.

Within the food exchange, you select the number of calories you will need to eat each day. We recommend women eat no fewer than 1,400 calories and men eat no fewer than 1,800 calories. Many men and women have reported they never went below these recommendations, and each week they still lost weight until they reached their goal weight. In First Place, we don't want men or women to lose over one and one-half to two pounds per week. The first one or two weeks your rate of weigh loss will be greater because you will have a water loss. Afterward, we know that if you lose more than two pounds per week, you are losing lean body mass. Lean body mass is your internal machine for energy and stamina. As a result, lean mass is not easily regained when lost. Within the First Place program, our goal is for people to lose only fat and not lean body mass.

Many people who begin the First Place program do not need to lose weight. These men and women experiment with the exchanges until they find the right number to maintain their weight. Most women can eat 1,800 to 2,000 calories per day and maintain their weight if they are exercising. The majority of men can eat 2,000 to 2,600 calories per day and maintain their weight if they are exercising. The goal of the program is for everyone to be eating healthfully. Some will consume fewer calories until the desired weight is reached, but everyone will participate in the same food plan.

Because First Place is a balanced food plan, pregnant women and nursing mothers can stay on the plan by simply adding some exchanges. If you are pregnant or have a medical problem of any kind, we advise taking our food plan to your doctor. Then the doctor can advise you on how much food and which foods to eat. In First Place we never attempt to be anyone's doctor; however, it is important to note that medical professionals designed our food plan.

What About Sugar on the Live-It Plan?
If people come into First Place and need to lose weight, we suggest they think about giving up simple sugar (the sugar found in cakes, pies and candy) until they reach their goal weight. We know that many people are addicted to sugar and that when you are on a reduced-calorie food plan, you don't need empty sugar calories. Each gram of sugar has four calories and absolutely no nutritional value. Honey has very little nutritional value also and is counted the same as sugar in First Place.

Sugar is not our enemy. If eaten in the right amounts, sugar is not a bad choice for occasional use. The problem is that we don't know what "right amounts" means. In 1900, Americans ate 6 pounds of sugar per year. The average is now over 140 pounds per year. That is 36 teaspoons per day. You might think to yourself, *Someone is eating my sugar!*—maybe not. Sugar has been found in 94 percent of all packaged foods. Check your labels. Here are some sample amounts of sugar:

Cola drink, 12 ounces	10 teaspoons
Ginger ale, 12 ounces	12 teaspoons
Fruit gelatin, ½ cup	4½ teaspoons
Cherry pie, 1 slice	10 teaspoons
Sherbet, ½ cup	9 teaspoons
Angel food cake, 4 ounces	7 teaspoons
Chocolate cake (iced), 4 ounces	10 teaspoons
Glazed donut	6 teaspoons

Unfortunately, because of the way food is processed, you can add sugar to your diet with little or no effort. It does take effort to monitor your sugar intake, and such monitoring is a key part of the Live-It plan.

Let's say [a teenager] starts her day with a "nutritious" breakfast of presweetened cereal. Mom is pleased she's eating cereal instead of a doughnut, but doesn't realize that one bowl contains 8½ teaspoons of sugar. That's a problem, especially when you add the 7 teaspoons in her white toast and jam, and the 6 teaspoons in the sweetened cider she washes everything down with. It's only 7:30 A.M. and she's had 21½ teaspoons of sugar! . . .

There's a midmorning break at school. Because Mom taught her well, she passes up the soda, but the chocolate milk she has instead adds 6½ teaspoons. At lunch time she enjoys a bowl of cream of chicken soup that has 4 teaspoons of sugar. A gelatin dessert adds another 4½, and a glass of presweetened lemonade contributes a whopping 8½ teaspoons. . . .

On the way home, our growing young lady passes a convenience food store. Since her lunch was light, she stops in for a snack. No big deal. Just a package of frosted chocolate cupcakes and a soda—and 23½ more teaspoons of sugar! . . .

That evening, Mom's too busy to cook, so she fixes a frozen beef dinner, complete with fries and catsup. That's another 5 teaspoons, and a small dish of ice cream adds 8 more. (At least she didn't serve cherry pie à la mode. One piece would have added an unbelievable 20 teaspoons of sugar.) Her total for the day: 81½ teaspoons of sugar—on a diet sadly representative of how many young people eat.[2]

If you look at the information, it's not too far from how many of us used to eat before we entered First Place!

Sugar eaten in the correct amounts has not been found through research to be harmful for most people. The phrase "eaten in correct amounts" is where Americans have a problem.

What's First Place's Position on Sugar?
We believe in following the recommendations of the major health organizations. Sugar is neither a "good" food nor a "bad" food. However, when it comes to a healthy eating plan, sugar provides calories but little in the way of nutrition. When trying to achieve and maintain a healthy weight, it's a good idea to cut back on sugar in favor of more nutritious foods such as fruits, vegetables and whole grains. Many First Place members have found success by eliminating processed sugar from their eating plan. If a member is meeting their body's nutritional needs and maintaining a healthy weight, moderate amounts of sugar can be included in the eating plan. You have to decide what's best for you. While not addictive, sugar has been found to trigger binge eating in some individuals.

There are many names for sugar, and Americans are eating a lot more than they think. In First Place we ask you not to eat any product that lists sugar as one of the first three ingredients. Ingredients are listed on labels by weight, so the ingredient that weighs the most is listed first and the other ingredients are listed in descending order by weight. Sugar is a little different on many labels because there are so many different names for sugar. By reading the labels and recognizing the terms, you can know how much sugar is in your food. Manufacturers have found that if they list the ingredients under the different names of the sugars, then they can list the actual sugar further down in the list. You might see items such as corn sweeteners, fructose, sucrose or sorbitol listed before sugar. These are just different names for sugar, and sugar would probably be second on the ingredient list if they were all lumped together.

There are great benefits from removing simple sugar from your eating plan. Have you ever eaten an orange immediately after a piece of pecan pie? That orange will taste completely different when you have not eaten foods high in sugar. All fruits taste better and vegetables seem to have more flavor when sugar is eliminated.

America has over 14 million diabetics. Research says that sugar doesn't cause diabetes, but one of the precursors to diabetes is obesity. How many Americans are obese because of the amounts of sugar and fat they consume? Even though research has not proved conclusively that sugar is addictive, we have heard numerous stories from participants in First Place that eating even small amounts of sugar causes them to want more. For many, the hunger level is intensified. Sugar and fat also tend to be binge foods for many people.

Each cell in your body and much of your total health is affected by your food choices. The goal in First Place is to provide your body (God's temple) with the nutrients needed each day to obtain the best health possible.

What About Sugar Substitutes?
Nonnutritive sweeteners can give you the taste of sugar without the calories. Even though foods made with nonnutritive sweeteners may be low in calories, many of them may also be low in nutrition. In a healthy eating plan, calories are not the only issue—you need to consider nutrition such as vitamins, minerals, phytochemicals and fiber.

In First Place, we have a keyword when it comes to sugar substitutes—"moderation." Most research is inconclusive about the long-term effects of sugar substitutes on our bodies. We recommend a total of no more than 20 calories from the "free foods" category. Be aware of your daily total calorie count from food products containing artificial sweeteners, including diet drinks. Also, consider the amount of artificial sweetener you add to food. Remember: moderation.

Decide what is best for you. Let your overall goals of achieving and maintaining a healthy weight and good health help you decide what is best for you. If you have concerns about any sweeteners, choose from the free foods that don't contain sugar substitutes.

How Do You Read Those Labels?
When it comes to food purchases, Americans are obsessed with the term "no fat." The term gives us permission to buy cookies and cakes since we think they don't contain fat or calories. The truth is that most no-fat desserts have more sugar that their fat-loaded counterpart. If you read the labels, sometimes the fat-free product has more calories than the identical product that is not fat free.

Most of us don't take the time or energy to read labels, but in First Place we emphasize the importance of understanding exactly what you are eating each day. The following are among the most common and potentially misleading claims:

1. *Percent fat-free*. Consider a frankfurter that claims to be 80 percent fat free. Unfortunately, when a label says a product is 80 percent fat free, the words refer to the weight, not calories. The frankfurter is 80 percent fat free by weight but contains 130 calories and nearly 80 percent fat! This claim is true not only for frankfurters but also throughout the supermarket. For example, one 97 percent fat-free yogurt is only 3 percent fat by weight but 24 percent fat by calories. To resolve this confusion, look past the "fat free" advertising to the nutrition label on the side or back of the package or can. See how many grams of fat are in a serving; then decide if you want to include the product in your reduced-fat diet.
2. *Lite*. For most products monitored by the USDA—meat, poultry and products that contain significant portions of those

items—"lite" means the product is at least 25 percent lower than similar products in calories, fat, sodium or breading (the label must state the exact nature of the reduction). When it comes to food regulated by the FDA, the term doesn't have to mean anything at all since that agency has yet to give the word a legal definition. Be warned about potential misuse of this label.

3. *No cholesterol*. This is one of the most misleading terms in the supermarket and is found on everything from cooking oil to potato chips to peanut butter. None of those items ever had any cholesterol. Cholesterol is found only in foods that come from animals and in palm oil and coconut oil. These "no cholesterol" products do, however, contain relatively high amounts of fat, which has the potential to be even harder on the heart than cholesterol!

4. *Natural*. A natural product monitored by the USDA has no artificial flavors, colors, preservatives or synthetic ingredients. It is minimally processed as well. What "natural" means on an FDA-regulated label is determined by the manufacturer.

5. *No sugar added*. This term is particularly confusing. First, it is different from "sugarless" or "sugar free." Both of those terms indicate that a product does not contain any table sugar (sucrose) or any of several other sweeteners, such as honey. But the food may have sugar substitutes such as sorbitol, which contains as many calories as sugar but does not affect blood sugar in the body the same way sucrose does. Sugar-free chewing gum and mints fall into this category. Items with no sugar added can have sucrose and other sugars as long as they are in the food naturally and have not been added to it.

The bottom line in First Place is that five grams of fat in any product except meat or a meat substitute equals one fat exchange. Check the grams of fat, not the percent of fat. Remember that labels on products constantly change, and new and more detailed information is constantly being added to the label.

Another item not on the First Place plan is alcohol because, nutritionally, it falls into the same category as sugar. If you were going to count alcohol on the exchange plan, it would have to count as sugar or fat. Since sugar has no nutritional value and fat has nine calories per gram, alcohol is not a healthy choice for anyone wishing to lose weight.

What If We Stray from the Food Plan?

We realize that from time to time people eat foods not on the food plan. The difference between our philosophy and that of many other diet plans is that when we make a choice that is not the best for us, we are not off the program. This food is listed but not counted on our Commitment Record, and at the next meal, we get right back on the program. Our old diet mentality told us that if we ate a candy bar or fattening dessert, we had to skip the next meal. When we did this, we were doomed to failure. Since we felt like a failure, we usually ate everything else in sight before returning to our healthy food plan. In First Place, we know that now and then a bad choice doesn't make us a bad person. Food has no inherent value, good or bad. All food is good; but in many cases, our preparation of these foods is not good for us. In First Place, you will be able to eat the same foods your family has always enjoyed. You will just learn to prepare them in a different manner, using more spices and removing the fat. Also, we have many wonderful desserts in First Place that contain no sugar. Our members are never deprived of any food; they can choose any food to eat. The key is to learn proper serving sizes, so you can be knowledgeable about how much food you're actually consuming. Many members tell us that they have served an entire First Place meal to guests and that their guests loved every bite. Often our mind-set about what is good food, and what is not, is totally unrealistic. We can educate our taste buds to prefer nutritious low-fat foods. It takes only a little more work than did our previous manner of preparation.

Why Do We Need to Lower Our Fat Intake?

If you read through the food exchanges in the Live-It plan, you will notice that First Place is a low-fat program. Since we usually aren't really careful, most of us consume more fat than we need.

Jim started with breakfast—a three-egg, ham and cheese omelette—and heaped 7 teaspoons of fat on the plate. He added 6 more for two slices of buttered toast, and 1 more for a glass of milk. He didn't even suggest bacon or ham because they are 90 percent fat and ought to be outlawed! . . .

Then Jim piled on 5 more teaspoons for a midmorning doughnut, and wondered how many men would stop at just one. Imagine what a glob of fat a long morning break could add! His lunch was chicken à la king—7 teaspoons of fat—and more bread and rolls, which added 3. He assumed the average working man would pass up an afternoon snack, but thought he would probably enjoy an all-American dinner: roast beef with mashed potatoes and gravy. For three ounces of meat, Jim loaded on 8 teaspoons, and for potatoes and gravy, another 5. Roll and butter, salad dressing, and cake with frosting each meant 3 more. A glass of milk added 1. The day's grand total was 50.[3]

Why Is Drinking Water Important?

Besides the Live-It food plan, we aim to drink at least eight glasses of water each day. If you have a 32-ounce insulated mug, you need to drink two of these each day. While it sounds incredible, water is quite possibly the single most important catalyst in losing weight and keeping it off. Most of us take water for granted, but water may be the only true "magic potion" for permanent weight loss. Here are a few of the many reasons it is important to drink water for your weight loss:

1. *Water aids in the digestion and absorption of foods and nutrients by suppressing the appetite naturally and helping the body metabolize stored fat.* Studies have shown that a decrease in water intake will cause fat deposits to increase, while an increase in water intake can actually reduce fat deposits. The reason this occurs is that the kidneys can't function properly without enough water. When they don't work to capacity, some of their load is dumped onto the liver. One of the liver's primary functions is

to metabolize the stored fat into usable energy for the body. So if the liver has to do some of the kidneys' work, it can't operate at full throttle. As a result, it metabolizes less fat, more fat remains stored in the body, and weight loss stops.

2. *Drinking enough water is the best treatment for fluid retention.* When the body gets less water, it perceives a threat to its survival and begins to retain every drop. Water is stored in extracellular spaces (outside the cells) and the storing is exhibited as swollen feet, legs and hands. The best way to overcome water retention is to give your body what it needs—plenty of water; then the stored water will be released. If you have a constant problem with water retention, then excess salt may be to blame. Your body will tolerate sodium only in a certain concentration. The more salt you eat, the more water your system retains to dilute it. It's easy to get rid of unneeded salt: drink more water. As water is forced through your kidneys, it takes away excess sodium.

3. *Water aids metabolism* An overweight person needs more water than a thin person because larger people have greater metabolic loads. Since water is the key to fat metabolism, it is logical for the overweight person to need more water.

4. *On the average, a person should drink eight eight-ounce glasses (about two quarts) every day.* However, the overweight person needs one additional glass for every 25 pounds of excess weight. The amount you drink should also be increased if you exercise briskly or if the weather is hot and dry.

5. *Water preferably should be cold.* We know that cold water is absorbed into the system more quickly than warm water. Some evidence suggests drinking cold water can help burn calories.

6. *To use water most efficiently during weight loss, drink water throughout the day.* In an ideal situation, a person drinks a glass or two of water at a time. Space these drinks out over morning, noon and evening.

7. *When the body gets the water it needs to function optimally, its fluids are perfectly balanced.* If you stop drinking enough water, your body

fluids will be thrown out of balance again; and you may experience fluid retention, unexplained weight gain and loss of thirst.

As you begin eating and drinking the First Place way, you will never want to return to your old habits. You are in for a treat, not a trial. In your quest for healthy living, drinking plenty of water should be a top priority. In fact, if you're currently not drinking enough water, *it's one of the significant lifestyle changes you can make.*

COMMITMENT 8: COMMITMENT RECORD

Commit to the LORD whatever you do, and your plans will succeed (Prov. 16:3).

As a participant in First Place, every day you fill out a Commitment Record (see Appendix B for an example of this form). Essentially a Commitment Record is a food diary plus a record of the completion of your other commitments. On it, you record not only what items you eat but also the amount of the items. This record allows you to record your difficulties with food and your victories over food temptation. Your completed CR shows exactly which foods you lack and which you overeat. The CR reveals what you are doing and what you are failing to do in all the nine commitment areas. Every good, sound weight-loss program has some method of keeping a record of your progress.

Keeps Us Honest

When I became a leader, I wasn't filling out my CR each day. During the leaders' meetings on Wednesday nights, I tried to reconstruct my food consumption over the previous week. During one of these meetings, Dottie Brewer said, "It's kind of hard to reconstruct a whole week in five minutes, isn't it, Carole?"

I got the point! Even today, many years after starting First Place, I find it helpful to keep a CR , so I stay on the Live-It plan. If I don't keep a CR, I have trouble sticking to the plan.

At your weekly group meeting, you turn in your Commitment Record to your leader for evaluation. Then the CR becomes a method of communication between you and your leader. Accountability is stressed in the program, not so your leader can judge or criticize you, but to encourage you to make good choices. One of our leaders refers to the CR as her best friend. This single form captures each one of the nine commitments as a helpful daily reminder. Consider your CR as a good friend. (If you do not attend a First Place group, find someone to share your CR with to keep yourself accountable.)

Accountability keeps us on track. When we write those sugary desserts on our Commitment Record, it keeps us from wanting to eat them. Anytime we eat something that is not on the program, we need to record it on the CR. In the past, you may have been on diet plans where if you ate a candy bar, you skipped lunch to stay within your calorie count for the day. In First Place, if you eat a candy bar or anything with sugar in it, you still record it on the CR. At your next meal, practice good nutrition and eat healthfully. This habit sets your mind on doing the right thing. While you may have exceeded your calories for the day, that's not going to make a great difference if you don't routinely stray from the plan.

Reveals Trends

We can hide so much from ourselves. For example, we may be eating larger amounts than needed. When we measure and weigh our food portions, the truth is revealed to us. John 8:32 tells us, "The truth will set you free." In this particular passage, John was not speaking about food. Nonetheless, the truth about what we eat, how much we eat and why we eat can free us from our bondage to food.

Every day your body needs 45 different nutrients. Fourteen hundred calories is the minimum you can eat to get these nutrients. If you don't eat all of the foods on the exchange list, you're going to lack some of the vitamins and minerals you need. Some of these nutrients the body does not store, so our daily food intake is vitally important to good health.

Omitting foods from any category turns First Place into another fad diet. You need a variety of foods on your CR. The beauty of the exchange program is that you find food in each group on the exchange list that you like to eat. You are not obligated to eat food you dislike. Each of you should go through the exchange list with a highlighter pen and mark all the foods that you like to eat. The highlighted areas will reveal either the wide variety or the limited nature of your choices.

Next try adding some of the foods you didn't highlight originally. Through the food exchange, many people have discovered new food choices. Asparagus, not a popular choice for everyone, was found to be high on one member's list when his wife prepared asparagus casserole. Other not-so-popular foods become edible choices for many of us as we learn that fruits, meats, grains and vegetables have distinct tastes. Many of us have eaten foods covered with butter, cheese or cream sauce for so long that we think everything should taste that way. You will enjoy the discovery of new tastes.

In addition to your food choices, you record the amount of water you drink. Your body needs at least 64 ounces of water every day. This amount is the equivalent of eight eight-ounce glasses. If you are like many people who are not water drinkers, it is important to drink an adequate amount of water for good health. Some of us have used colas, fruit juice, tea and other beverages to quench our thirst. Knowing the need for water and the effect of not having enough water can help us form the habit of drinking more water daily. When our body is used to consuming more ounces of water, we will have the desire for it.

Reinforces Our Commitments

While recording the foods we eat is an important component of the CR, the form is also designed to show where we are on the other commitments. On the CR you record when you've read your Scripture, had your prayer time and encouraged another member of your class. This section also asks about your type and length of exercise. This ongoing record reflects the extent to which you are keeping your commitments. These commitments are actually more important than which foods you eat. If you keep these commitments, eventually your food choices will fall into line. Then you can get stronger and become more committed to your Christ-centered health program.

Sometimes you may fail to start your Commitment Record on the first day of the week, or you may skip a day or more—you may even skip a week! If you attend a group and you don't fill out a CR, we ask you to put your name on a CR and write a note to your leader explaining why you didn't fill it out that week. Your leader will want to know why you're not doing one of the commitments, so he or she can pray for you. Whether you have a reason or an excuse, you need to have somebody pray with you about it, so your next week will flow a little smoother. Sometimes there are definite reasons for not doing a CR for the week. We are not looking for perfect people in First Place, just committed people.

Many people keep their Commitment Records in their Bible study. Others find that keeping it in their purse or organizer—even posted on the refrigerator—is more convenient. The CR is a valuable tool to help you, so you should use it in the best possible fashion.

After you reach your goal weight, you don't have to fill out a Commitment Record; however, many of my leaders who are at their goal weight continue to fill out a CR every week. They find that filling out a CR is helpful in maintaining their weight. It guides us in making correct choices in all food groups. When you increase your calorie intake after you get to your goal, you will find the CR to be a regular reminder of what led to your attaining your goal.

If this concept is new to you, then you are going to find that as you fill out your Commitment Record, God will be providing the answers that you have sought for so long. Give the Lord permission to change your life through your commitment to fill out a CR.

COMMITMENT 9: EXERCISE

Do you not know that in a race all the runners run, but only one gets the prize? Run in such a way as to get the prize. Everyone who competes in the games goes into strict training. They do it to get a crown that will not last; but we do it to get a crown that will last forever. Therefore I do not run like a man running aimlessly; I do not fight like a man beating the air. No, I beat my body and make it my slave so that after I have preached to others, I myself will not be disqualified for the prize (1 Cor. 9:24-27).

Exercise is the last of the nine commitments, and, I believe, one of the most significant. As I have said, these commitments are not ranked in order of importance because each one works in tandem to bring our lives into balance. Exercise is one of my personal favorites though, because it has changed my life in many different ways.

The Unenthusiastic

Many of you will love the exercise commitment, but many of you will exercise and never develop a love for it. Even if you don't love to exercise, I can assure you that you will love the way you feel after exercise. My assistant, Pat Lewis, reached her goal weight without ever exercising. For over 30 years Pat and I have been friends, and we used to lead a noon First Place class together. She never liked exercise and never found the time for it. Several years ago, while attending another church, Pat joined my early morning First Place class. Often to tease me Pat would bring me articles that said exercise was bad for you, or that reported that someone had died while exercising. When Pat reached her goal, people in her church began to ask her to lead a First Place group. As a leader, she felt guilty about never exercising herself. As a result, Pat prayed that God would work out a way for her to begin exercising. A few years ago, Pat started working at the First Place headquarters, which is about 25 miles from her home. Before long, Pat found that if she left at 7:00 A.M., her drive to work took over an hour; but if she left at 6:00 A.M., she could zip in on the freeway, have time to exercise, shower, get dressed and still arrive at work before 8:00 A.M. Then, when her daughter had her first child, Pat stayed with her for a week. Afterward Pat reported that if she hadn't been exercising regularly, she would have never had the stamina to do her work during that occasion. Pat will tell you that she still doesn't love to exercise, but she loves the way it makes her feel.

There are a few things about exercise that I don't like myself. One is, I don't like to sweat. Sweating wouldn't be so bad except that my hair gets wet and I have to wash it every day after exercising. But exercise has become as daily as brushing my teeth and going to work. I can promise you that my day goes better when I go ahead and exercise than when I choose not to exercise. As I recall that 80 percent of life is showing up, I am motivated to exercise, even when I can't muster any enthusiasm. Also, since only 5 percent of the population exercises on a regular basis, if you exercise three to five times a week, you join an elite group of people.

The Exercise Commitment

The exercise commitment asks that you exercise three to five times a week aerobically and incorporate flexibility and strength training into your lifestyle as well. Aerobic exercise can be any exercise that elevates your heart rate to a training level and keeps it there for 20 minutes. We have included a chart in Appendix C that will show you what your training heart rate should be during exercise so that you know if you are in the training range. Aerobic exercise might include walking, jogging, swimming or bicycling. While aerobic exercise is important, there are two other components of exercise which are equally as important: flexibility and strength training.

Exercise Aids

The following are either necessary or helpful as you seek to establish a regular exercise program:

1. *A good pair of shoes.* From my perspective you don't need to spend a lot of money to exercise. Although it is possible to spend as much on your exercise clothes and shoes as the rest of your wardrobe, all you really need are some loose fitting pants, a shirt and a pair of comfortable shoes. Cost is not an indicator of whether a shoe is right for you. The critical factor is locating a shoe that fits: one that is not too wide, too short or too long. Serious exercisers do not look like they stepped out of a fashion catalog; usually they look pretty grubby—but they are comfortable. Don't wait to start until you get everything perfect. Start with what you have, and God will bless you.

2. *Walking.* In October 1984, I began walking and after I could walk a mile in 15 minutes, I began jogging. While running is never necessary to attain a good fitness level, I began running because it takes less time to run three miles than to walk them. We burn 100 calories for every mile covered, whether we walk slowly, walk quickly, jog or run. The goal is to work up to at least three miles per day. You can decide how fast you will cover those three miles. If you are just beginning your exercise program, you might think, *Three miles! I can barely walk to the car.* In the early days of your exercise commitment, if you can barely walk, then barely walk. Before long you will discover that your stamina improves and you can increase your distance to three miles. Chapter 10 includes the testimony of Beverly Henson, who could barely walk when she started exercising. Read it and be inspired to begin walking today.

3. *Exercise log.* I keep a personal log of when and how much I exercise. If I miss a week, I just write across that page what was going on and why I couldn't exercise. At the end of the year, my goal is to never exercise less than I did the year before. That way I am always working to increase my fitness. For your convenience and to help you get started, a sample exercise-log page is included in Appendix C.

4. *Christian cassettes and CDs.* Every day when I exercise I use the First Place Scripture memory CDs. I find that when God's Word goes into my mind for an hour each morning, then the Lord can bring it out when I need it. Many times during the night when I wake up, I find myself reciting a verse of Scripture I learned while exercising or singing one of the Scripture memory songs. What we listen to most is what will be in our subconscious when we sleep. That may be a scary thought for some of us, with all the garbage we allow to invade our minds. Use your exercise time to praise God and memorize His Word.

5. *Pulse monitor.* For my birthday, my husband, Johnny, gave me a pulse monitor, which monitors my heart during exercise. It has a band that goes around the rib cage and a watch that picks up

the heart rate. With this pulse monitor, I don't have to stop and take my heart rate during exercise. I can glance at the watch and if it is too slow, I speed up; if it is too fast, I slow down. Pulse monitors can be purchased at any sporting goods store, but they are not essential for exercising. If you haven't been exercising, it won't take over five or ten minutes for you to reach your training heart rate. My pulse monitor helps me, however, because I have been exercising for many years, and I had grown lazy. I had a hunch I wasn't working hard enough and the monitor proved it! For me, the monitor has been as motivational as my exercise log was when I first began to exercise.

Workout Times

My best time to exercise is in the morning because fewer people need me early in the morning. If you have young children, the morning might be your worst possible time to exercise. Several years ago I went to my son's home after dinner to visit. His wife, Lisa, had gone to his office building, where they had an exercise room, to work out, and John, my son, was watching their three little ones. After trying different workout times, Lisa has found that with three active children, an early morning workout before John leaves for work is best. You will need to experiment and find the time of day that works best for you. The main thing is to choose a time you can stick with on a regular basis.

Many young parents use their children as an excuse not to exercise. Yet children love to go out and walk and ride bikes. There is no better family time than when the entire family exercises together. It thrills me to see moms and dads out exercising with their children. These children are learning a lifetime habit.

Husbands and wives have also told me that they never had time to truly communicate with each other until they began exercising together.

Some singles have met their spouses while working out. Exercise is good for any age and at any time. The main thing is to pick a time when you can be faithful to exercise. If you can exercise regularly after work, then that is fine. Some studies have revealed that if we work out in the late afternoon, we are less hungry at dinnertime. Afternoons have never worked for me because there are too many things that come up unexpectedly to deter my efforts.

Dr. Couey has done studies with women who couldn't lose weight as a result of years of yo-yo dieting. Their metabolism was so low that they were stuck and couldn't seem to lose any weight. Dr. Couey discovered that if these women broke their exercise into two or three times a day, it jump-started their metabolism. For instance, if you normally walk for one hour, then walk 20 minutes morning, noon and night. This arrangement also works when you have lost weight and have hit a plateau. Beverly Henson's testimony in chapter 10 talks about trying this method of exercise to shock her metabolism into action.

Organizational Abilities

Exercise has many benefits beyond strengthening our hearts. One of my greatest benefits has been to become a more organized person. It defies explanation, but I can plan and organize while I exercise better than at any other time. I have never been an organized person and have always resisted being organized. After I started exercising, I began to receive some of my best ideas while working out. I could solve problems that seemed unsolvable. Scientists tell us that our endorphins kick in when we have exercised for about 45 minutes. If this is true, then it makes sense that our mental cobwebs begin to clear and we start to think better after exercising. Some of us need this more than others!

Senior Adults

As we grow older, we often think that we just don't feel well enough to exercise. But amazing things happen when senior adults start exercising. You have probably read stories of seniors who could barely walk, and now they are running marathons and going mountain climbing. I don't personally know any of these people, but I do know countless senior adults whose lives have been changed—and even saved—by the exercise commitment.

For example, my mother at age 76 planned to go with our family on a beach vacation when we rented a beach house. All of my children and grandchildren were there, along with my sister, her children and her grandchildren. On July 4, the men were busy barbecuing while the women sat and visited. My mom began to feel sick and went inside to lie down. My mom never lies down unless she is extremely ill. Within an hour, her fever was very high. My brother-in-law checked Mom and said we needed to take her to the hospital. On Independence Day you can imagine how crowded we found the hospital emergency room. At 2:00 A.M. we finally got Mom into a room. Her temperature had soared to 106 degrees. She was diagnosed with streptococcal septicemia, a strep infection of the blood that usually kills people within 12 hours. This same infection killed Jim Henson, creator of the Muppets. Fortunately, we were at a teaching hospital and my mother received excellent care. She had 8 to 10 doctors around her day and night. They were amazed that she was able to survive this raging infection that usually kills much younger people. Although hospitalized for 10 days, she recovered. To my amazement, the doctors told Mom if she hadn't been a faithful walker, her heart wouldn't have been strong enough to withstand that type of infection.

I use this story to stress that the time to get physically fit is now—not when you are suddenly ill. Then it is too late. When you are well is the time to get fit, even if you are not as well as you would like. If you think you're not well enough to exercise, you must start where you are right now. Begin by walking a short distance every day. God will begin to strengthen your body. My mom is no longer able to walk for exercise because of arthritis in her spine, and she is in a wheelchair, but she will tell you of the importance of exercise at any age. My mom is now in her late 80s and she still does exercises to strengthen her arms and legs so that she will continue to have the strength to stand up and to sit.

I could continue touting the benefits of exercise for several more pages, but I'll stop here. Please make sure you turn to Appendix C and check out the extra resources. When you exercise on a regular basis, it will change your life. The only way to find out is to put on those shoes and walk out your front door!

We've completed the nine commitments and you have learned the basic program of First Place. In the next chapter, we'll discuss the additional programs within First Place such as Fitness Weeks, conferences and additional training workshops. We continue our journey to a Christ-centered life.

✳

CHAPTER EIGHT

BEYOND THE BASICS

Linda Kelley started attending a First Place group at First Church of Dover, Florida. Invited by her best friend, Sylvia Montefu, who had lost 40 pounds, Linda wanted to lose weight and restore her energy and stamina. A Christian for many years, Linda now celebrates her deeper walk with God through the First Place program.

Linda and some other women from her church attended a First Place conference in Hollywood, Florida. To describe her experience at the conference, Linda says, "There was quality content and excellent information which was presented with humor, love and conviction. I especially enjoyed Beth Moore as a role model and godly woman, along with Dr. Dick Couey, who, as a well-known physiologist from Baylor, could present medical information in layman's terms."

FIRST PLACE CONFERENCES

Once you've learned the basic program of First Place, you have learned the foundational elements. However, within First Place there is a program much broader than the initial groups. First Place conferences are held throughout the year in different locations, such as Nashville, New Orleans, Cincinnati or Dallas. There are no prerequisites to attending a

First Place conference. Some of the participants are leaders in First Place who want to receive additional training, while others simply want to learn more about the program or a specific commitment. Leaders and their class members often attend these events to enrich their lives spiritually, emotionally, mentally and physically. However, many people who attend our conferences have never been in First Place but want to learn about the program. Conference participants attend a wide selection of seminars that address spiritual and emotional growth, as well as seminars that teach members how to take care of their bodies. Participants also enjoy a number of dynamic speakers such as Beth Moore, Florence Littauer and Dr. Dick Couey (professor of physiology from Baylor University in Waco, Texas), among others. The atmosphere at these conferences is electric and the fellowship with other Christians is a boost to your spiritual life. An added plus is the opportunity to eat First Place meals and discover firsthand how wonderful these recipes can be. For specific dates and times, contact First Place.

FITNESS WEEKS

Besides the First Place conferences, several times a year First Place offers a Fitness Week program at Round Top, Texas. The times and speakers vary. The week-long conference includes inspirational messages, exercise time, praise and worship, and devotionals. These in-depth meetings give participants a chance to interact with various leaders of First Place and get their questions and concerns answered individually. More than anything else, these Fitness Weeks are spiritual experiences that boost the life of each participant.

Some time ago, Dianne Stone from Greensboro, North Carolina, attended a Fitness Week. She decided to attend the conference during a time when she felt a great deal of stress from her life, job, son and her First Place commitments. She was starting her second session of First Place and had lost 30 pounds. Now Dianne was beginning to feel burned out, so she planned to give her commitments a boost with a Fitness Week. A week before the conference, Dianne reinjured her knee and had surgery for a torn cartilage. She contemplated delaying her Fitness Week until another session but decided to press ahead.

During the first two days of the Fitness Week, Dianne suffered with a migraine headache. As she says, "I was not a happy camper, but by Sunday, things were looking up." One aspect of that particular Fitness Week was to participate in a social fast with time alone with the Lord. Dianne says, "I was able to rekindle a love relationship with Christ." For Dianne, her time at Fitness Week was invaluable.

Another participant, Missy Deterling, also talked with me about her experience at Fitness Week. Like Dianne, Missy brought her own struggle to the week—an allergy infection which persisted the entire time she was there, so she coughed and felt sluggish. The highlight for Missy wasn't the excellent food, the exercise or the terrific teaching—while she raved about each of these aspects. She says, "The reason to participate in Fitness Week is for a spiritual renewal, a camaraderie with like-minded Christians and plenty of free time to spend with the Lord. I came away with such a peace, a stronger commitment to my Lord and a renewed attitude knowing that I can do all things through Christ who strengthens me" (see Phil. 4:13).

FIRST PLACE WORKSHOPS

If you want additional help learning the First Place program or want to know how to begin and lead a First Place group or program in your church or community, call our office to find out about a First Place workshop in your area. Workshops are now offered all around the country. The purpose of the workshop is a passion to see the ministry grow, and each one is hosted by a church with an active First Place program. Each workshop teaches such topics as the history of the program, the four-sided goals, the nine commitments, the mechanics of starting a program, what it takes to be a leader, meeting procedure and the food plan. A First Place workshop may be a good way to learn more about First Place and to give you the tools to begin a program where you live. Workshops are usually held on a Saturday from 9 A.M. to 2 P.M.

ADVANCED TRAINING FOR LEADERS

We offer workshop leader certification for First Place leaders who have led for two years. This training equips leaders to organize and teach First Place workshops in their geographical region. Advanced leadership training includes six hours of classroom instruction and an evaluation of each trainee's presentation skills. After this training, a leader must plan and present a First Place workshop in his or her area, observed by a First Place representative. After a satisfactory evaluation, the leader becomes a Certified Workshop Leader.

MONTHLY NEWSLETTER RESOURCE

First Place also has a monthly First Place newsletter that provides inspiration, motivational articles, fitness information, recipes, articles about nutrition and fitness, as well as conference, Fitness Week and workshop information. Each month's issue features an inspiring testimony with before and after photos. The newsletter is available for a reasonable fee. To order, contact First Place.

APART WE CAN DO NOTHING

The additional resources listed in this chapter help you continue First Place as a lifestyle, instead of a short-term program. Our emphasis is to help you live in Christ abundantly. Jesus said in John 15:5, "I am the vine; you are the branches. If a man remains in me and I in him, he will bear much fruit; apart from me you can do nothing."

This is a key to my life: Apart from God and Jesus Christ, I can do nothing. Throughout this book, I've given you many tools and guidelines, but apart from God's help for every step, you cannot succeed. With God's help, you can live in a manner that pleases Him. He may plan for you to lead a small First Place class. God knows your life and heart and whether you will participate or lead a class.

Class size is no indicator of the success of your efforts or of what God is doing. Some classes remain small, while others continue to multiply themselves in numerous areas around the original group. We lovingly accept those God has given us and leave the results from First Place in God's capable hands. We do the work of God, but He brings the results.

During the last several years, I have become aware of God calling out to me, "Don't just do something, stand there." You see, I want to do things for God in a proactive manner. The Lord appreciates my availability, yet He wants me to come to His throne of grace through prayer and continued trust in Him. As I do so, He guides my life day to day. He will do the same for you. You are not alone in First Place—except by choice. The First Place staff is readily available to help you with a wide variety of seminars and resources. We look forward to serving you in the days ahead.

Do you have dreams for your future? Let's explore our future and God's plans for us in the next chapter along our journey to a Christ-centered life.

❊

CHAPTER NINE

A DREAM FOR TOMORROW

In October of 1984, I sat with a friend at a women's retreat at a church camp near Austin, Texas. I didn't know anything about the speaker, but many people have heard her since that time—Patsy Clairmont. She had recently started her speaking career and talked about carrying a little notebook she called her dream notebook. During this retreat, Patsy talked to the group about having dreams.

As I listened, I wondered what sort of dreams could fill my life. At that time, I had never spoken anywhere to any group, yet there was a tiny seed of a dream in my heart to do so. At the commitment time during the retreat, I prayed, "Lord, if You want to do something with this dream, I'll make this promise: If I'm ever asked to go anywhere to speak, if I can possibly say yes, I'll say yes." As soon as I returned to my office, the invitations began. Some of them were unusual. Once I spoke in a home where I sank so deep into the sofa that I couldn't see my notes. Yet these small meetings allowed me to do something some call the PIT—Putting In Time. Anybody with a dream has to go through the PIT in order to train and gain experience before the dream becomes a reality.

What are your dreams about your future? In the earlier chapters of this book, I detailed how you can lose weight and improve your spiritual life as you follow the nine commitments of First Place. You've learned a great deal about nutrition and read the personal stories of a few real people who have already made this same journey. These people found more than weight loss through First Place—their lifestyle was radically changed and their relationship with the eternal God was strengthened. My hopes and expectations are great for you. Is God placing some dreams in your heart? Are you willing to put in the time—to undertake the hard work, training and pain that are necessary for those dreams to become a reality?

Some of you reading these pages have already been through great pain because of your physical appearance. Your self-confidence is pretty low, and your mental image of what is possible may be pretty small. Maybe your spiritual relationship is weak, and you've rarely prayed or read your Bible on a consistent basis. Or possibly you begin breathing hard when you think about walking up some stairs because the idea of exercise is frightening.

In this chapter, I want you to consider the words Paul wrote the church at Ephesus: "Now to him who is able to do immeasurably more than all we ask or imagine, according to his power that is at work within us" (Eph. 3:20). According to the *King James Version*, Ephesians 3:20 says that God "is able to do exceedingly abundantly above all that we ask or think." I have a vivid imagination and can dream up some amazing things—yet God in His great love is able to do more than I can think or imagine.

As you look to the future, I want you to consider three major points. First, you need to see beyond the obvious; then you need to pray beyond the possible; and finally, you need to live beyond the temporary.

SEE BEYOND THE OBVIOUS

The Bible is filled with examples of ordinary people who were completely committed to God's leadership in their lives. Consider the life of Noah and the fact that Genesis 6:8-9 (*KJV*) says, "Noah found grace in the eyes of the LORD. These are the generations of Noah: Noah was a just man and perfect in his generations, and Noah walked with God." It took years of discipline for Noah to build the ark. His entire life focused on obeying God and building a huge boat—on dry land. If you are going to follow the nine commitments of First Place and change your lifestyle, it will involve adjustments and discipline. You will need to find some discipline you may not possess right now—except in your dreams.

Before my involvement with First Place, I didn't have discipline in my life. I drifted from day to day, just seeing what fun thing I could be involved in next. Through First Place, I've been able to fulfill many of my dreams, but it took many daily adjustments and the pain of discipline. In 1987 when I started my role as First Place national director, I could not envision the growth of our organization. I could not envision myself committed to the disciplines of prayer and exercise. I had to see beyond the obvious.

Consider the great patriarch Moses. Face-to-face, Moses met with God so much that his countenance glowed! If you recall, Moses was a reluctant leader. When he was tending sheep in the Midian desert and went to investigate a burning bush, God spoke and called him to return to Egypt to free the Israelites. Moses had every excuse as to why he could not lead the people. Finally he said he couldn't speak well, so God permitted his brother Aaron to go with him. Later, however, when Moses was on the mountain receiving the Ten Commandments, Aaron allowed the creation of the golden calf.

Yet despite Moses' mistakes, God used him. One time I heard an older woman use the expression "Just let him whup himself." God allows us to "whup" ourselves a lot if we are determined to act on our own energy and strength. If you want to lose weight through First Place and have tried other things on your own strength, maybe you've "whupped" yourself. You must let go and let God take over your life. He will use your life if you look beyond the obvious.

Or consider Jonah. He refused to listen to God and fled to Tarshish. God wanted Jonah's life and commitment, so the Lord created a huge storm, and the sailors threw Jonah overboard. A giant fish swallowed him, and after three days, he was willing to go to Nineveh and preach repentance. After God released Jonah from the belly of the fish, he obeyed God and preached in Nineveh. The people in the city repented and turned to God. Then Jonah was mad because God answered his prayers but not in the manner that Jonah wanted. The prophet had wanted the people of Ninevah zapped by God, but they repented. In our lives, our prayers are often not answered as we would like them to be. God isn't some puppet on a string that we manipulate to meet our whims and desires. He answers our prayers for change in His way, according to His will, and for His purpose in our lives. I pray that you will take your plans related to First Place and put them at the foot of the Cross—where all ground is level—and ask God to help you see beyond the obvious.

PRAY BEYOND THE POSSIBLE

As you dream about your future and a healthy lifestyle, I hope you will also begin to pray beyond the possible. Prayer is our communication link to our heavenly Father. As the eternal God, He sees the beginning and the end of our months, our years and our lives. My finite mind tries to figure out what God will do in a particular circumstance. But Isaiah 55:8,9 says, "'For my thoughts are not your thoughts, neither are your ways my ways,' declares the LORD. 'As the heavens are higher than the earth, so are my ways higher than your ways and my thoughts than your thoughts.'" From these verses, I know that God will not respond in the ways that I sometimes think He should respond. My job is to honor God with my prayers and listen for His direction as I read the Scriptures. The most wonderful part of this is that God's ways and thoughts work perfectly at the perfect time.

Through First Place, we have given you a solid program for a lifestyle transformation: physical, mental, emotional and spiritual growth. I have no idea how God will work in your life, but I'm confident that He will work in all of these four areas if you will make the vow to persevere and not quit until you possess the victory. When we put God in first place, then He can help us pray beyond the possible. I hope you will place your complete trust in God as He helps you pray beyond what you can see for your future. If God had shown me what my future would become in First Place when I started in 1981, I would have balked and said, "It's too hard and there's no way I can live up to those standards and commitments." God in His patience leads us one step at a time. Possibly you have been through a tremendous struggle in your life and don't feel like you can pray beyond the possible. Romans 8:26,27 says that the Holy Spirit intercedes for us when we don't know how to pray. Ask the Holy Spirit to pray for you and take your petitions to our heavenly Father. The days ahead will brim with excitement in your life. I'm personally excited for you as you take this step of faith and trust God to continue working in your life through His power and might.

LIVE BEYOND THE TEMPORARY

Finally, I hope you will live beyond the temporary. Our world is looking for the easy way out and the quick solution. Many of us have tried the quick weight-loss methods and the results have been temporary. Our weight has returned. The basis of First Place is a total lifestyle change. As you follow the nine commitments, then God transforms you to move beyond the temporary into a total change of lifestyle.

In January 1988, shortly after I became the national director for First Place, I read 1 Corinthians 9:24-27:

> Do you know that in a race all the runners run, but only one gets the prize? Run in such a way as to get the prize. Everyone who competes in the games goes into strict training. They do it to get a crown that will not last; but we do it to get a crown that will last forever. Therefore I do not run like a man running aimlessly; I do not fight like a man beating the air. No, I beat my body and make it my slave so that after I have preached to others, I myself will not be disqualified for the prize.

As I read this passage about running the race called life, God drew my attention to the final verse of this section: "No, I beat my body and make it my slave so that after I have preached to others, I myself will not be disqualified for the prize." This final verse has become one of my life verses. It helps me live beyond the temporary and follow the discipline of a Christ-centered lifestyle.

Many people tell me, "After the first of the year, I'm going on a diet." Why wait? Why not begin tomorrow? Oswald Chambers, in *My Utmost for His Highest*, explains that our battle is fought in our will.[1] Most of us have stubborn wills that resist God's direction and plans for our lives. The Lord wants to transform our lives mentally, spiritually, physically and emotionally. Still, many of us are lazy and living for a temporary solution. We must remember that we can do all things through Him who gives us strength (see Phil. 4:13).

Through the pages of this book, you've started the journey of a lifetime. It's not temporary and it begins with a single step, as the testimonials in the next and final chapter will prove. So let me congratulate you for taking not only that first step but also for all the steps to come. Above all, follow the key principle of First Place—put God in first place in every aspect of your life.

✳

CHAPTER TEN

FIRST PLACE IN MY LIFE:
PERSONAL TESTIMONIES

CATHY DRESSLER
NEWPORT NEWS, VIRGINIA

Throughout my life, there have been specific days that have altered the course of my life. The day I became a Christian, the day I was married, the days of the births of my three children, the date I was diagnosed with Parkinson's Disease.

I had just celebrated my 35th birthday when I received the formal diagnosis of Parkinson's Disease—an incurable, degenerative neurological condition. It was April 10, 1991, and I was devastated. Since the word "Parkinson's" had first been spoken in connection with what was "wrong with me," I had read all I could find about this relentless disease. I wanted to break down. But all those who know my character and my strong faith wouldn't allow me to fall apart. I repeatedly heard, "If anyone can handle this, you can." Finally I did fall, broken in heart, broken in spirit, crying out to my heavenly Father. In His infinite love and care, He wrapped His arms around me and lifted me up. I was reassured by

His promise that I would be healed—whether in this earthly life or in paradise with Him, I would be healed.

Soon both sides of my body were affected by symptoms of Parkinson's—tremors, rigidity, overwhelming fatigue and, in my case, pain. I had to resign from the job I loved—teaching preschool. Through it all my faith stood strong. Walking became an effort as I concentrated on picking up one foot after the other. I began to drag my left foot so badly that I would often stumble, mostly catching myself, yet sometimes falling. Still, God would not let my spirit fall; His words "I am with you!" were my constant companion.

Orthopedic shoes and leg braces were ordered by one of my doctors at the National Institutes of Health. The brace literally lifted my foot from the ground as I walked, and the shoes allowed room for the brace

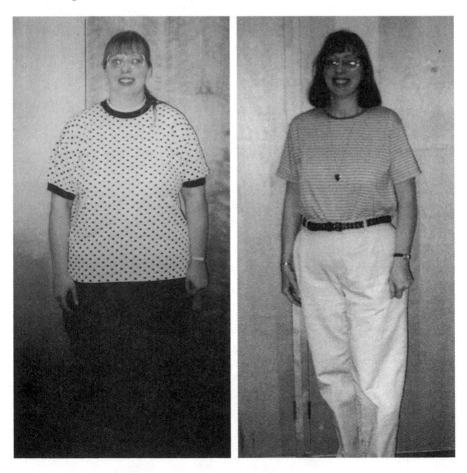

but also eased the pain caused by dystonia of my foot. Walking was still a tiring effort.

Already extremely overweight, I began to gain even more weight as inactivity characterized each day. But I felt that my eating was at least one thing I could control. I could still eat what I wanted, when I wanted, even if I couldn't do the other things I enjoyed. Little did I realize I was not in control of my eating; it was in control of me.

But that all changed on the next momentous day in my life: June 11, 1996, the date of my first First Place meeting—the day I turned my body over to God. I had turned my life over to Him, my family, even my disease. Everything changed! Food became what I needed—fuel for my body, not an answer to fluctuating emotions. I started to do home-bound exercises. But my determination to walk grew and grew. Just three weeks after I started First Place, I walked my first mile. It took 45 agonizing minutes, but I did it!

Then it happened. On a balmy summer evening, as I walked with my husband, a verse from my First Place Bible reading that day was brought to mind. The verse from Proverbs 4:12 says, "When you walk, your steps will not be hampered; when you run, you will not stumble." Over and over the Holy Spirit spoke those words to me: "You will not stumble. You will not stumble." With each step my feet felt lighter, freer. Then, almost of their own volition, they picked up speed, my stride lengthened, and I was running! I ran for three blocks! My husband called out, "Go, girl!" and his words intermingled with the sound of my Father saying, "I am with you!"

I have now lost 93 pounds and over 30 inches on the First Place program. I'm now leading my second session and being blessed by each class member. I get so excited when someone asks how I lost the weight, just the opening I need to tell them what God has done for me through First Place. I praise God and give Him the glory for every pound lost, every inch gone, every step taken.

Oh, and those orthopedic shoes and the leg brace are now relegated to a dusty corner of my closet. This past Christmas, my wonderful husband gave me a new pair of shoes. What kind? Nike Air Windrunners, of course!

Sharon King
Effingham, South Carolina

For as long as I can remember, I struggled with a food and weight problem. Little did I know that January 1995 was the beginning of the end of the struggle. In December 1994, after regaining a third of 20 recently lost pounds, I admitted defeat in the weight war. I decided I would not put myself through the mental and emotional torture of another diet—even if it meant weighing over 200 pounds.

Yet everything changed a few weeks later, when I saw a poster in my Sunday School class advertising First Place. As I read and reread the information about this new program of discipleship training, I knew God wanted me to participate. I could also sense I would have a major role in it, even though I couldn't begin to imagine what God had in mind. I com-

mitted at that moment—sight unseen—to whatever the program required. Early in the program I was quickly convicted that the First Place lifestyle was what the Lord wanted me to live the rest of my days. He wanted me to follow the Live-It plan—to exercise and to be in a daily personal relationship with Him through prayer and the Word. Through the nine commitments, I learned my problem was a spiritual problem. I'd never made the connection before, but food and appetite were false gods. Food separated me from God because I turned to it for comfort instead of to Him. In the past I had questioned Him—why did He make me this way? I didn't believe He could help me. Today I shudder when I think that I was willing to accept that defeated, unfulfilled lifestyle. Thank the Lord He doesn't give up on us even when we do.

It has been almost six years to the day since First Place became a part of my life. It is still so fresh and exciting. To me the First Place lifestyle is the one Jesus modeled and I've been called to "live it" every day. I continue to grow spiritually, mentally and emotionally, while maintaining a healthy weight and size.

The question I am most often asked is, "Do you still do Commitment Records?" The answer is, "Yes!" Filling out a Commitment Record is a small thing to maintain a healthy, happy, energetic and balanced life. These daily records pave the way to overcoming a lifelong struggle and are necessary to having total health.

Jesus touched me and continues to touch me through the First Place program. Through the Bible, prayer, good nutrition, exercise and the group members, God is helping me to be a better follower of Jesus and to guide others to do the same. People look at my before pictures and comment, "You don't look like the same person." I'm not—praise God!

PAULINE W. HINES
FIRST PLACE DIRECTOR
NEW ORLEANS, LOUISIANA

I was introduced to the First Place program by a coworker. She asked if I'd be willing to try the program and I said, "Why not! I've tried everything else—why not try Jesus!" And the rest is "His-story"! I learned through First Place that Jesus Christ is the perfect example of total wellness. His story unfolding in our lives allows Him to be Lord over every area—mental, physical, spiritual, emotional. Giving Him complete control allows Him to give us life, in abundance, *before* we get to heaven.

The First Place ministry offered me an incredible support system through encouragement, fellowship and an awareness of habitual strongholds—those empty places we so often fill with over- and under-eating. Over time those empty places were filled by Jesus Christ. And seeking Him and His righteousness first has had its rewards. I am now 110 pounds lighter. Yet the physical baggage I have shed does not compare to my amazing loss of the excess inward baggage I had always car-

ried. God is so good! And to Him I give the glory for the life-changing victories I have experienced in First Place.

JIM CLAYTON
PASTOR, DIXIE LEE BAPTIST CHURCH
LENOIR CITY, TENNESSEE

Seventy pounds overweight. High blood pressure. A spastic colon. Shortness of breath. That was me in August 1993, when my wife and some ladies in the church where I was pastor introduced me to Carole Lewis, Kay Smith and First Place. At 42 years of age, I had become a terrible example and a poor witness.

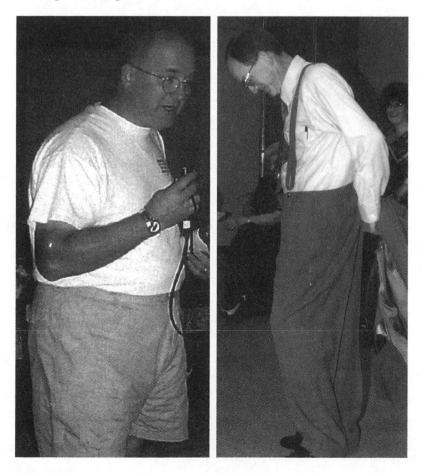

Almost eight years have now passed, and First Place has absolutely changed my life. My weight and blood pressure are under control (no medication), the colon problems are gone, and my "temple" has become a much more acceptable place for Jesus to dwell in.

Over the past eight years, there was a brief time following my knee surgery when I got away from the First Place commitments. The weight began to return, accompanied by the health problems and the lack of discipline. But, praise the Lord, through His grace and guidance, I am now back where I want and need to be, striving every day, in every way, to put Jesus in first place in every area of my life.

CHERYL CORTINES
JACKSONVILLE, FLORIDA

I turned 40 last year and my life flashed before my eyes. I thought to myself, *Life is passing me by.* Why, you ask? It was all about the numbers: my weight and my age. I knew I had to do something but what? I had tried every diet from A to Z. Sure, I would lose some weight, but as soon as I got off the diet, I would go back to my old eating habits and gain everything back, sometimes more. I was tired of living like this.

In December of 1999 my pastor asked me if I would be interested in teaching a First Place class again (I had done so three years previously). I knew I wanted to lose weight and I thought that maybe this would motivate me, so I said yes. I knew that being the teacher would mean that I would have to practice what I preached. Then I thought to myself, *I work a full-time job, I'm a mother and wife, and I'm an active church member. How will I be able to prepare my meals, study my lesson, prepare for teaching the class, exercise, etc.* The list went on and on. Then I remembered something I had heard at a seminar. People find time for what is important to them no matter how busy they are. And you know what? They're right. I realized my excuses were just that—excuses. I was setting myself up to fail before I had even begun.

This time I was prepared to give up anything for my goal. I know that God does not give us a dream that we can't obtain. Yes, there will be obstacles, but without them we can't grow. I had to learn how to take care of myself. It seemed that I always put myself on the back burner, while everyone else came first. My first goal was to make *me* top priority. I knew that if I didn't, I might not be around much longer to enjoy my family and friends. My second goal was to lose weight so that I could do the things that I really enjoyed but wasn't able to do now. I had to constantly remind myself of my goal. I made a magnet to put on my refrigerator that said, "Don't give up what you want most for what you want at the moment." Believe me, I read that a lot and it really did help.

On January 1, 2000, I started back on First Place. By May I had lost 60 pounds and by January 2001 I had lost 130 pounds. I always considered myself a happy person, but I had no idea how much happier I really could be. God truly has changed my life. What a miracle! I actually enjoy exercising now. Walking is a big stress reliever for me and I do it all the time. Through the First Place lessons, I learned that I can have control over my own life and have the power to believe in myself just like God does. That is truly priceless. I know that losing the weight is only half the battle and keeping it off is the other half. But I know that I can do all things through Christ that strengthens me (see Phil. 4:13).

Everyone asks me how I lost my weight. My answer is that there are no shortcuts! Think positively, eat nourishing foods, exercise daily, drink your water, and, most of all, pray (a lot)! Know that God can do amazing things in your life through First Place.

I spent 20 years waiting for a miracle diet or pill and guess what—it never came and it probably never will. First Place isn't about going on a diet, losing weight and then going back to your old habits. It doesn't work like that. This is for the rest of your life.

Life is like a coin: You can spend it any way you wish, but you can only spend it once.

ANGIE PATTERSON
KINGWOOD, TEXAS

He will not let your foot slip—he who watches over you will not slumber (Ps. 121:3).

My story is probably typical of a lot of longtime churchgoers. I became a Christian at an early age and grew up going to church. I was involved in everything the church had to offer. I was well educated in the Christian life, so I thought I knew what I was supposed to do concerning God's will in my life.

However, I have struggled to maintain my weight my whole life. As I was growing up, I was described as "pleasantly plump." That statement always seemed to be a contradiction; I didn't see anything pleasant about being plump. As a young adult I was always within my weight range, but it was a struggle. During that time I got away from church and started

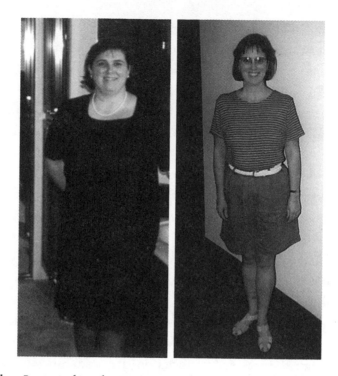

doing what I wanted to do. However, I began to feel that something was missing from my life.

When I married my husband, Bill, we started going to church; but I carried with me the attitude I had developed as a young adult: *I can do it all and I don't need God for everything, especially in the area of food and weight control.* I know that thought came directly from Satan to keep me stranded where I was spiritually.

The downward spiral with my weight gain started after Bill and I were married. There were the pressures of a new marriage, dual careers and graduate school. During that time we started to depend on convenience food for our meals. Our meals consisted of prepackaged fatty food from the grocery store and Domino's pizza. Although I was shocked to realize that we spent $1,200 per year on pizza, we didn't stop eating it. I just switched to buying pizza in the grocery store where it was cheaper but still high in fat.

For the next 10 years I gained about eight to ten pounds a year.

The beginning of the end was in October of 1995. Bill and I planned a vacation to Estes Park, Colorado—one of God's great creations. We had not had a vacation together for about four years and we were really looking forward to the time together. However, when we got to Estes Park, we could not do anything without being winded and extremely tired. We told ourselves it was the elevation, but it wasn't. All we could do was drive around the valley floor. I wanted to be on the mountaintop—and I think God wanted me on the mountaintop, so I could be closer to Him.

During that trip it really hit home that I was too young to be that out of shape. There were still a lot of mountains to climb—not just physically but spiritually also. At that time I could not physically climb any mountain. After the trip, I started watching what I ate and lost nine pounds in four months, which is an acceptable weight loss. However, at that rate, it would take me years to get to a reasonable weight. That was an overwhelming thought.

During that time some ladies at my church started talking about a program called First Place. I was always leery of structured weight-loss programs since they seemed to focus on the food. Since food was the problem, how could focusing on the food be the solution? Besides, I knew everything I needed to know about nutrition and how to run my life.

When First Place started at our church, Bill and I went to an orientation and we were surprised at what we heard. Soon after beginning the first Bible study, *Giving Christ First Place*, I was convicted that overeating was disobedience to God. This was a very painful revelation to me. Disobedience in one area of your life pulls you down and away from God's will for your life. God then revealed to me that *all* areas of my life needed to be turned over to Him.

I lost 95 pounds in 14 months. I thank God for allowing me to see His power in my life. I continually remind myself of Romans 9:21, "Does not the potter have a right over the clay, to make from the same lump some pottery for noble purposes and some for common use?" The Potter is here to mold us. Christian life is better without a spiritual tug of war on how we are molded.

Since losing weight with First Place, I have had three opportunities to experience hiking on a mountaintop: the Grand Tetons, Wyoming;

Estes Park, Colorado; and the Canadian Rockies. With my feet and God's power, I made it to the top. God is faithful; He *will* bless your efforts.

BILL PATTERSON
KINGWOOD, TEXAS

When I came to First Place, I was confident that I was a Christian—yet there was a huge gulf in my life. I never read the Bible and only prayed when I was forced to do so. We regularly attended church, but I had no active faith.

Weight loss was the major reason I joined a First Place group. I didn't know how to eat, and when it came to convenience food, I was worse than

everyone else, eating bags of chips and fried food. Food was essential for any celebration—a birthday, Christmas or just getting together with friends. Although I had been heavy most of my life, I wasn't sure exactly how heavy until I joined a First Place group.

It had been almost 10 years since I had stepped on a scale. I even skipped regular physical exams because I knew the nurse would want to weigh me. I knew my weight would be around 300, but I had no idea it would be 310 pounds the first night. Like many people, I wanted to deny there was a problem with my weight.

I started the program in June 1996 along with my wife, Angie. Both of us have lost weight and are maintaining our weight-loss goals. I went from 310 pounds to 185 pounds in a little over 10 months' time. And people have noticed. Because I now look so different from my driver's license picture, I get a lot of questions at the airline ticket counters. "What happened to you?"

I've had the opportunity to tell thousands of people about what Christ has done in my life. Before First Place I was introverted and lacked self-confidence, both in my work and in my witness for Christ. Now, after losing my weight, I've shared my testimony on Christian radio and at churches and conferences around the country. I have also shared what God has done in my life in the business world, motivating hundreds of my peers to improve their health and in many cases improve their walk with the Lord.

I have also realized that God had a very special plan when He led me to First Place. I was raised in a non-Christian home. My parents were not against religion. They just never had a need for it. But that began to change when mom and dad came to Houston for Christmas the year we joined First Place. They saw our change and were stunned! When they asked how we did it, we gave the credit to the Lord, and for the first time in my parent's lives they saw the power of Jesus Christ. That Christmas week my nearly 80-year-old parents opened their hearts to Jesus. Nine months later in a church in Grand Rapids, Michigan, my mom and dad walked to the altar and accepted Jesus Christ as their Lord and Savior.

JOE ANN WINKLER
SHAWNEE MISSION, KANSAS

I want to let you know how thankful I am for the First Place program. I am not just thankful for the weight loss but also for what First Place has done for me in other areas of my life. For years, I had not been able to find my place in church ministry. I had always been very shy and afraid to attempt anything.

All of that began to change for me when I joined a church that was just starting a new First Place group. I got information about the pro-

gram and decided to join if my daughter would go with me. I loved First Place from the start and began assisting in a class after my first session.

Because of my husband's job, I had to move from Kansas to Iowa. I tried to find a First Place group, but there were none in the area and my new church did not want me to start one. I decided to remain a member of my group in Kansas, staying in touch through the mail. I couldn't make my phone call, but I did write someone in the class every week to encourage them. After 15 months, we were able to move back to Kansas, and I was able to get right back into a group. Since my leader had other commitments and was going to discontinue the class, she asked if I would take over the group, and I agreed.

That was three years ago. In March of 1995 I received my First Place leadership training certificate, and today I enjoy holding workshops to train new leaders. I have also organized a monthly leaders' get-together, in which we share new ideas, discuss problems and fellowship with each other. I publish a weekly newsletter for my First Place group and that of another church. I now spend three full days each week on First Place. While my work is almost like a job, I love it too much to call it a job. It is my *ministry*.

I am not shy anymore. I have lost 115 pounds, and I love First Place. It has changed my life and enabled me to help others change theirs. When I look at myself—a woman with multiple sclerosis who is confined to a wheelchair most of the time—I am reminded that God can use "broken vessels" to do His will. What a wonderful Savior we have!

DR. MARK BENEDETTO
SIOUX FALLS, SOUTH DAKOTA

I was first exposed to First Place during the fall of 1995 while serving as vice president of student services at East Texas Baptist University (ETBU) in Marshall, Texas. Two staff members of ETBU, who were enrolled in First Place at their local churches, achieved impressive success. Possessing both a personal and university-wide interest, I enrolled

in First Place through Pine Crest Baptist Church in Longview, Texas. Intrigued at the possibilities of integrating the program into the 15-week semester and motivated by my rapid weight loss (42 pounds in 13 weeks), I developed a unique strategy for the implementation of First Place on the university campus.

But getting started wasn't easy. I had to really pray for a spirit of boldness and also a spirit of sensitivity in presenting the First Place information to our students. This was especially true with the presentations in the female residence halls, as most meetings were held during the late evening hours and at times I was the only male in the building!

Yet things did eventually come together. We installed display racks in the cafeteria to provide additional information about the First Place program and to expose readers to the First Place newsletter. At the beginning of the fall semester, I led seminars in each residence hall to explain the First Place program to the nearly 800 students living on campus. To facilitate an immediate visual recognition, I installed a First Place food station in the cafeteria serving line. The station was outfitted with a sign, featuring the First Place logo to attract attention and to identify the non-fast-food options for students. The campus food services provider prepared most of the entrees by using the First Place recipes, serving over 200 people each day.

Students and faculty/staff, as a group, shed more than 500 pounds, exceeding their established team goals for combined weight loss. More importantly, though, students were excited to hear that whether they achieved weight loss or remained at the same weight, the First Place program was designed to help them lay a foundation for a spiritual fitness plan.

I hope that the First Place program at ETBU is the catalyst for the establishment of additional First Place programs on other college campuses, and that someday First Place will be added to the health and fitness curriculums and offered for college credit.

I still live by the principles of First Place—and I hope my testimony will help others as much as First Place has helped me.

BEVERLY HENSON
MERIDIAN, MISSISSIPPI

Thanks be to the Lord for leading me to First Place. This past year has been one of the most exciting years of my life. A year ago, I had just about given up all hope of ever being healthy again. I weighed 273 pounds; I was unhealthy, I had tried and failed almost every diet program, and the devil had almost convinced me (at 45 years old) that I was washed up and destined to be a perpetual couch potato. Wrong! I asked God to help me, and He sent me to First Place.

For two sessions, I was faithful to keep all my commitments, but the weight did not come off. This had never happened to me before. On almost any diet, the scales would show a weight loss or weight gain. It seemed that the Lord had me on maintenance—I still weighed 273 pounds.

My First Place leaders encouraged me to go to the First Place conference in New Orleans and speak to Dr. Dick Couey, one of the seminar speakers at the conference. Before attending the conference, I wrote down my diet history and found that over the years I had lost almost 500 pounds *and* gained almost 800 pounds. At the conference, I was able to speak to Dr. Couey regarding my weight-loss problem. He then told me how to jump-start my metabolism. At that point, I could choose to either stay at the same weight, or I could choose to put forth the effort to get into shape.

The day after the conference, Sunday, February 8, 1998, I began walking six miles a day. I walked two miles in the morning, two miles at noon and an additional two miles in the evening. I did exactly what Dr. Couey told me and I walked faithfully for 18 weeks. I began to lose weight immediately! I walked through many miles of pain until I began to feel great and look forward to my daily walks. I soon realized that the Lord had given Dr. Couey the words to get me on the right path. I now realize that even at 45 years old, I can still lead an active life. At the end of the 18 weeks, I weighed 223 pounds—I had lost 50 pounds. Since jump-starting my metabolism, I can now exercise normally and lose more weight.

God has really been working miracles in my life. My beginning weight was 273 pounds. I am a new creature through the glory of God. In April 1999, I reached my goal weight of 150 pounds—a weight I have successfully maintained. Meeting my goal marked the end of a wonderful journey that had transformed me and started me on a new journey to learn how to maintain and sustain being a steward of good health. I am now a certified personal trainer and am able to encourage people to get out of that recliner and start moving into a healthier lifestyle.

I am truly walking in the abundant life that is promised by God. First Place has blessed me with the knowledge of God and given me the direction to move on through Him. It is truly a wonderful life! I give glory to the Father and thank First Place for a new direction.

Ron Dillon
Pastor, First Baptist Church
Mount Pleasant, South Carolina

I kept thinking that one day I would do something about it. A few years back, I told my wife I was going to diet and get in shape. Many times, when I would hear of a weight-loss plan that sounded good and easy, I would think of trying it. I was not able to stay on any plan even for one day.

I remember hearing of First Place and thought it might be different. I tried unsuccessfully to get some folks in our church interested in leading First Place, so I dropped the idea.

Gradually, as middle age crept in, and I grew heavier little by little, something had to be done. I asked God to show me a way to lose weight that I could accomplish with His help. I desired a healthy body that would be a more fitting image of a representative of Christ. Very soon after that prayer, I saw an ad for a First Place conference in our state.

I asked a deacon friend to attend with me. We went and were surprised at the program and the people we met. They were not fanatics. They were serious Christians who saw the body for what it truly is meant to be—a temple of the Holy Spirit. We came home from the conference with a commitment to start First Place.

With much fear and trembling on my part, we started a First Place program in April of 1994. Leading the Bible studies was actually enjoyable. And to my surprise, I was able to stay on the Live-It plan and lose weight. When I started the program, my weight was 260 pounds. By the end of October 1994, I weighed 188 pounds. Since then, I have maintained that weight and have continued leading First Place in our church.

First Place has been an answer to a prayer. Through the program God has greatly blessed me, as well as many others in our church and the

surrounding area. First Place is not a diet, but it has taught me a new way to eat for the rest of my life. I have discovered how to choose food that is healthy and tastes good. Regular exercise and strengthened spiritual disciplines are now part of my daily life. I could not have dreamt the joy and happiness God would bring to my life through First Place.

LIVE-IT: RECOMMENDATIONS FOR NUTRITIONAL HEALTH

Calories from the foods you eat provide the energy and nutrients your body needs for good health. They provide the fuel that powers your body mentally, physically and spiritually. The key to achieving and maintaining a healthy weight lies in calorie balance. Weight gain occurs when you take in more calories than your body needs. To lose weight, you must reduce the number of calories you take in or increase the number of calories you use up.

It's best to lose weight slowly. Low-calorie diets and rapid weight loss promote a slowing of the metabolic rate, which makes it more difficult to lose and maintain your weight in the long run. Studies show that exercise may be the most important factor in the maintenance of long-term weight loss. Regular physical activity may prevent the slowing of the metabolic rate that often occurs with weight loss. Also, it's very difficult to get all the nutrients your body needs each day when your calorie intake drops too low. Because physical activity burns calories, you can take in more calories from a healthy diet and still lose weight.

CHOOSING A CALORIE LEVEL

Use the following tables to help you choose a daily calorie level for healthy weight loss. Choose the recommended calorie level for your age and body weight. This calorie level is your starting point for the Live-It plan.

Recommended Calorie Ranges for Women					
Age↓ / Weight→	100-119	120-139	140-159	160-179	180+
20-39	1400	1400	1500	1600	1600
40-59	1200	1400	1400	1500	1500
60+	1200	1200	1400	1400	1400

Note: *If your goal is to maintain weight, add 300-500 calories to your plan.*

Recommended Calorie Ranges for Men					
Age↓ / Weight→	140-159	160-179	180-199	200-219	220+
20-39	1800	1800	2000	2200	2400
40-59	1600	1800	1800	2000	2200
60+	1500	1600	1800	1800	2000

Note: *If your goal is to maintain weight, add 400-600 calories to your plan.*

The tables use the best available methods for estimating a calorie level for healthy weight loss; however, your needs may be different. Age, gender, heredity, body size and physical activity influence the number of calories your body needs. It's best to lose weight at a rate of one-half to two pounds each week. Adjust the calorie plan up or down based on how you feel and how well you are meeting your goals. If you are losing more than two pounds a week, change to the next higher calorie level. Also, if you're not losing weight, check your portion sizes—many people don't realize how much they're eating!

A balanced diet and regular physical activity are the keys to good health and successful weight loss.

FIRST PLACE CALORIE LEVEL EXCHANGES

This daily exchange plan allows you to personalize your Live-It plan based on your nutritional needs and eating preferences. Choosing the lowest number of exchanges from each food group will give you fewer calories than listed. To stay within your calorie level, don't choose the higher number of exchanges from more than one food group. You can,

Daily Exchange Plans						
Levels	Bread/Starch	Vegetable	Fruit	Meat	Milk	Fat
1200	5-6	3	2-3	4-5	2-3	3-4
1400	6-7	3-4	3-4	5-6	2-3	3-4
1500	7-8	3-4	3-4	5-6	2-3	3-4
1600	8-9	3-4	3-4	6-7	2-3	3-4
1800	10-11	3-4	3-4	6-7	2-3	4-5
2000	11-12	4-5	4-5	6-7	2-3	5-6
2200	12-13	4-5	4-5	7-8	2-3	6-7
2400	13-14	4-5	4-5	8-9	2-3	7-8
2600	14-15	5	5	9-10	2-3	7-8
2800	15-16	5	5	9-10	2-3	9-10

Note: *The food exchanges break down to approximately 50-55% carbohydrate, 15-20% protein and 25-30% fat.*

however, choose the highest number of exchanges for the fruit and vegetable groups. Choose what works best for you.

The above Daily Exchange Plans allow you to personalize your Live-It plan based on your nutritional needs and eating preferences. Choosing the lowest number of exchanges from each food group will give you fewer calories than listed. To stay within your calorie level, don't choose the higher number of exchanges from more than one food group. You can, however, choose the highest number of exchanges for the fruit and vegetable groups. Choose what works best for you.

DESIGNING YOUR PERSONAL EATING PLAN

To design your personalized eating plan, take the following steps:

1. Choose your appropriate daily calorie level from the Choosing a Calorie Level table.
2. Choose your daily exchange allowance from the table above.
3. From your daily exchange allowance, record the total exchanges for each food group in the Live-It plan below.
4. Distribute your daily exchange allowances into the three time periods in your plan.

My Live-It Plan= _____ *calories*				
	Calorie Level			
	Morning	Midday	Evening	Totals
Bread/Starch				
Vegetable				
Fruit				
Meat				
Milk				
Fat				

USING THE FOOD EXCHANGES

Using food exchanges is a simple way to ensure proper nutrition. Dieticians and health professionals have used this method for many years. You can use exchanges for losing weight, gaining weight or maintaining a healthy weight. People can also use food exchanges to regain health lost by years of poor nutrition.

The term "food exchange" doesn't need to be intimidating. Foods are divided into seven exchange lists: Bread/Starch, Vegetable, Fruit, Meat, Milk, Fat and Free Foods. Each food list contains similar amounts of proteins, fats, carbohydrates and calories.

All the foods within a food list contain approximately the same amount of nutrients and calories per serving, which means that one serving of a food from the bread list may be exchanged (or substituted) for one serving of any other item in the bread list. For example, a bread exchange can be one of the following:

- one tortilla
- one and one-half cups of puffed cereal
- one-third cup of peas

By using food exchanges in your daily eating plan, you are always able to choose foods you like that fit your lifestyle.

Food exchanges will

- encourage variety
- assure well-balanced meals
- make menu planning easier
- help establish permanent lifestyle change.

HELPFUL HINTS FOR LIVING-IT EVERY DAY

Breakfast—Why or Why Not?

Breakfast! Is skipping it really that bad for you? Is a good breakfast really all that important? The answer to both of these questions is yes!

Breakfast, the first meal of the day, usually occurs after at least an eight-hour fast. If you eat supper early in the evening, which is best, then the fast may be as long as 12 hours. A healthy body constantly maintains an appropriate blood sugar, or glucose, level so that you have an energy supply readily available for your daily needs. To work efficiently, you must maintain glucose levels. However, after a nightlong fast, your body will have to resupply the blood with glucose. If your body doesn't receive that nourishment in the form of a proper high-carbohydrate breakfast, then it must use the reserves it has stored in the liver. The constant withdrawal of your body's required amount of glucose each morning from your liver causes undue stress on the organ. Studies show that your mood and performance are affected by the foods you eat and especially by the lack of food. Certain mechanisms in the body, such as those which regulate appetite, fluid and electrolyte balance and neurotransmitter levels in the brain, are adversely affected by being deprived of the nutrition provided by a good breakfast.

The most common excuse given for poor work performance is fatigue. The most apparent factors of fatigue are inadequate rest and excessive work, but nutritional deficiencies can contribute to fatigue just as much.

Overall, poor eating habits diminish a person's abilities and can lead to exhaustion, apathy, poor concentration and reduced strength.

UCLA's Center for Health Sciences conducted a study which monitored approximately 7,000 men and women. They found that the men who "rarely or sometimes" ate breakfast had a 40 percent higher death rate than those men who ate breakfast "almost every day." They also found that the women who "rarely or sometimes" ate breakfast had a 28 percent higher death rate than those women who ate breakfast "almost every day." These statistics are surprisingly high to many people. No one can predict for you if you will be one of those who suffer seriously from not eating a good breakfast, but we can warn you that you place yourself in some risk if you don't. The University of Iowa did a long-term study that showed that better mental and physical performance among children and adults was directly associated with eating a nutritious breakfast. The subjects who ate breakfast were more productive and satisfied with their work performance during the late morning. Also, they had faster reaction times, which, in most instances, resulted in fewer accidents on the job.

One other risk is associated with skipping breakfast: You're likely to miss some very important nutrients, including vitamin C, thiamine (vitamin B), riboflavin (vitamin B_2), iron and calcium. These nutrients might be absent in the other meals of the day. Ninety-five percent of our food today is processed food and is low in essential nutrients. Going without breakfast only increases the chances that you won't consume all the essential nutrients your body needs.

Now that you know why it's bad to skip breakfast, what constitutes a nutritious breakfast? Bacon, fried eggs, buttered toast and coffee may taste good, but they aren't the best foods to choose. They constitute a high-fat breakfast, which gives you no advantage in starting your day. A good breakfast should average from 350 to 400 calories. These breakfast calories should be distributed as follows: 55 percent carbohydrates, 20 percent protein and 25 percent fat. Some people believe in consuming a large breakfast, but actually, consuming more than 25 percent of your day's calories for breakfast reduces overall efficiency.

A large breakfast is not needed, but a balanced or properly distributed breakfast is essential.

Remember, a good breakfast is essential for good health. Don't take the chance of ruining your health by skipping breakfast!

Live-It While You Eat Out
Below is a list of some simple guidelines to follow when eating out. With a little planning ahead of time, you can work the First Place program and enjoy eating out—at the same time!

- Appetizers often can serve as the entree.
- Request salad dressing on the side. Dipping your fork into the dressing will save a lot of fat.
- Carry oil-free dressing with you.
- Avoid all creamy salads. Starchy vegetables, creamy salads and meat salads are loaded with sugar and fat.
- Avoid marinated salads and pickled vegetables. They may contain sugar and fat.
- Choose only fresh fruit. Many canned fruits contain sugar.
- Select darkest greens available and add a variety of vegetables. Fresh spinach is an excellent salad base. Use spinach instead of lettuce, which provides very little nutrition.
- Select lean meat entrees. Request that they be grilled dry without fat or butter.
- Avoid all fried items.
- Request that all sauces or gravy be served on the side. They are often full of sugar or fat.
- Avoid casseroles and meat entrees in sauces. Chicken à la king, for example, averages 7 fats (35 grams) per serving.
- Be creative—lemon juice and picanté sauce are great on fish. You may want to carry packages of butter flavorings.
- Your hand can serve as a measuring device when estimating meat servings. The average palm equals a 3-ounce serving of inch-thick meat, the end section of your thumb a tablespoon, and the end section of your little finger a teaspoon.

- Beware of "dieter specials." Specify nonfat and sugar free when ordering! Many "diet" plates are full of fat and sugar.
- Split the entree and order an extra salad. If alone, ask for the entree to be divided in half and packaged in a carryout before it comes to the table.
- If you desire a substitution, ask for it, even when the menu states, "No substitutions." Restaurants usually are willing to accommodate special requests from regular customers.
- If something comes with your order that you do not want, ask the waiter to leave it off the plate.
- Request no butter or margarine on your bread.
- Request baked potatoes and pasta dry. Mention that "dry" means no added fat.
- Baked potatoes are great topped with steamed vegetables, picanté sauce, jalapeños, lemon juice and pepper, ranch dressing, steak sauce or cut-up meat. Be creative!
- Request skim milk for coffee.
- Fresh fruit is a good choice for dessert, or you might save a roll or bread to eat while others are having dessert.
- Fast-food restaurants are now serving low-fat choices. Ask if chicken can be grilled dry. Choose wisely!
- Enjoy the experience! Don't compromise your health and commitment!

Final Thoughts

Words of wisdom for those who have joined First Place to lose weight:

There is no magic potion for losing weight.

No gimmicks or gadgets can guarantee quick and easy weight loss.

An effective weight-loss plan needs to be both sensible and livable.

To get long-lasting results, this is what you need to do:

Eat less, exercise more!

Change behavior.

Use portion control.

Make sure your new habits become a permanent part of your lifestyle.

THE FOOD EXCHANGES

The six exchange lists, or food groups, were developed to aid in menu planning for First Place. The individual diet plan prescribed by a physician and/or registered dietitian indicates the number of servings from each food group that should be eaten at each meal and snack. The chart below shows the amount of nutrients and number of calories in one serving from each food group. If you cannot or choose not to eat from a particular food group, consult with a physician or nutritionist to insure proper nutrition.

	Carbohydrate (in grams)	Protein (in grams)	Fat (in grams)	Calories
Bread/Starch	15	3	trace	80
Vegetable	5	2	—	25
Fruit	15	—	—	60
Meat				
Lean	—	7	3	55
Medium Fat	—	7	5	75
High Fat	—	7	8	100
Milk				
Fat Free	12	8	trace	90
Very Low Fat	12	8	3	105
Low Fat	12	8	5	120
Whole	12	8	8	150
Fat	—	—	5	45

BREAD/STARCH LIST

Each item on the bread/starch exchange list contains approximately 15 grams of carbohydrates, 3 grams of protein, a trace of fat and 80 calories. The foods in this versatile list contain similar amounts of nutrients. The bread/starch list encompasses cereals, crackers, dried beans, starchy vegetables, breads and prepared foods.

Helpful Information About Bread/Starch Exchanges

- Watch for hidden fats.
- Cereals equaling 80 calories count as 1 bread/starch exchange.
- Choose bread/starch products containing less than 5 grams of

sugar (4 grams equals 1 teaspoon of sugar). Cereal or bread containing fruit will have added grams of sugar.

- Choose products high in fiber. (25-35 grams of fiber per day is recommended.)

	Carbohydrates (in grams)	Protein (in grams)	Fat (in grams)	Calories
Bread/Starch	15	3	trace	80

CEREALS, GRAINS AND PASTA

Barley (cooked)	⅓ cup
*Bran cereals (concentrated)	⅓ cup
*Bran cereals (flaked)	½ cup
Bulgur (cooked)	½ cup
Cooked cereals	½ cup
Couscous (cooked)	⅓ cup

HIGH FIBER CEREALS

Grape-Nuts	3 tablespoons
Grits (cooked)	½ cup
Kasha (cooked)	½ cup
Millet (cooked)	¼ cup
Other ready-to-eat unsweetened cereals	¾ cup
Pasta (cooked)	½ cup
Puffed cereal	1½ cups
Rice (white or brown, cooked)	⅓ cup
Rice (wild)	½ cup
Shredded wheat	½ cup

DRIED BEANS, PEAS AND LENTILS

*Baked beans	¼ cup
*Beans and peas (cooked) such as pinto, kidney, white, split, black-eyed	⅓ cup
*Lentils (cooked)	⅓ cup

ALTERNATIVE EXCHANGE

*Beans, peas and lentils	1 cup = 2 bread + 1 lean meat
Flour, soybean	½ cup = 1 bread + 2 meats + 1 fat
Miso	½ cup = 1 bread + 2 meats + 1 fat
Tempeh	½ cup = 1 bread + 2 meats + 1 fat
Wheat germ (toasted)	¼ cup = 1 bread + 1 lean meat

STARCHY VEGETABLES

*Corn	½ cup
*Corn-on-the-cob (6" long)	1 ear
Hominy	½ cup
*Lima beans	½ cup
*Peas, green (canned or frozen)	½ cup
*Plantain	½ cup
Potato (baked)	1 small (3 ounces)
Potato (mashed)	½ cup
Pumpkin	¾ cup
Squash, winter (acorn, butternut)	¾ cup
Yam, sweet potato (plain)	⅓ cup

BREADS

Bagel ½	(1 ounce)
Bread, lite (40 calories per slice)	2 slices
Bread sticks (crisp, 4" long x 1.2")	2 (⅔ ounce)
Croutons (low fat)	1 cup
English muffin	½
Frankfurter or hamburger bun	½ (1 ounce)
Pita (6" across)	½
Plain roll (small)	1 (1 ounce)
Raisin (unfrosted)	1 (1 ounce)
*Rye, Pumpernickel	1 (1 ounce)
Tortilla, corn (6")	1
Tortilla, flour (6")	1 + ½ fat
White bread (including French and Italian)	1 slice (1 ounce)
Whole-wheat bread	1 slice (1 ounce)

CRACKERS AND SNACKS

Animal crackers (1 ounce low fat, low sugar)	1 bread + ½ fat
Graham crackers (2" square)	3 squares
Matzo	¾ ounce
Melba toast	5 slices
Oyster Crackers	24
*Popcorn (air-popped with no fat added)	3 cups
Potato chips (baked)	1 ounce
Pretzels	¾ ounce
Pudding (sugar free made with nonfat milk)	½ bread, ½ milk
Rice cakes	2 regular, 6 mini
Rye Crisp, 2x3½ inch	4
Saltine Crackers	6
Tortilla chips (baked)	1 ounce
Vanilla wafers, 8 low-fat wafers	1 bread + ½ fat

BREAD PREPARED WITH FAT	
Count as 1 bread/starch serving, plus 1 fat	
Biscuit (2½")	1
Chow mein noodles	½ cup
Cornbread (2" cube)	1 (2 ounces)
Cracker, round butter type	6
French fried potatoes, 2-3½" long	10 (1½ ounces)
Hummus	¼ cup
Muffin (plain, small)	1
Pancake (4")	2
Rolls (butter style)	1
Stuffing, bread (prepared)	¼ cup
Tabouli	2 tablespoons
Taco shell, (6")	1
Tortilla chips	5
Waffle (5x½")	1

COUNT THESE AS 1 BREAD/STARCH AND 2 FAT EXCHANGES:

Baking chocolate	1 ounce
Corn chips	1 ounce
Croissant	1 small (1 ounce)
Grape-Nuts	3 tablespoons
Potato chips	1 ounce

The following are equivalent to one bread exchange, although many are not as nutritious as other selections from the bread exchange group.

MISCELLANEOUS	
Barbecue sauce	¼ cup
Barley (dry)	1½ tablespoons
Bran (raw, unprocessed)	½ cup
Bread crumbs (dried)	2 tablespoons
Catsup	¼ cup
Chili sauce	¼ cup
Cocoa	5 tablespoons
Cornmeal	2½ tablespoons
Cornstarch	2 tablespoons
Flour (all varieties)	2½ tablespoons or 1 cup = 5 bread exchanges
Malt (dry)	1 tablespoon
Tapioca	2 tablespoons
Tomato paste	6 tablespoons
Tomato sauce	1 cup
*Wheat germ	3 tablespoons
Yogurt (frozen nonfat)	3 ounces

* 3 grams or more of fiber per serving.

VEGETABLE LIST

Each item on the vegetable exchange list contains 5 grams of carbohydrates and 2 grams of protein. Each exchange is 25 calories. The generous use of assorted nutritious vegetables in your diet contributes to sound health and vitality. Enjoy them cooked or raw.

Helpful Information About Vegetable Exchanges

- Eat a minimum of 2 vegetables a day. Three to four vegetable exchanges are encouraged.
- Fresh, frozen or canned vegetables are all good choices.
- You get more nutrition and fewer calories by munching on fresh vegetables. Keep your refrigerator well stocked with ready-to-eat vegetables.
- Prepare vegetables by grilling, steaming and stir-frying. Avoid fried vegetables.
- Any fat added during preparation must be counted.

	Carbohydrates (in grams)	Protein (in grams)	Fat (in grams)	Calories
Vegetable	5	2	—	25

VEGETABLES
Unless otherwise noted, the serving sizes for vegetables (one exchange) are: 1/2 cup cooked vegetable or vegetable juice; 1 cup of raw vegetables

Artichoke (12 medium)	Asparagus
Bamboo shoots	Beans (green, wax, Italian)
Bean sprouts	Beets
Broccoli	Brussels sprouts
Cabbage (cooked)	Carrots
Carrot juice	Cauliflower
Eggplant	Greens (collard, mustard, turnip)
Heart of palm	Italian green beans
Jicama	Kale
Kohlrabi	Leeks
Mushrooms (cooked)	Okra
Onions	Pea pods
Peppers	Pimento (3 ounces)

Rutabaga	*Sauerkraut
Shallots (4 tablespoons)	Snow peas
Spinach (cooked)	Summer squash
Tomato (one large)	*Tomato/vegetable juice
Turnips	Water chestnuts

FREE VEGETABLES:
Raw, 1 cup

Alfalfa sprouts	Bok choy
Cabbage	Celery
Chinese cabbage	Cilantro
Cress, garden	Cucumber
Endive	Escarole
Green onion	Hot peppers
Lettuce	Mushrooms
Parsley	Radishes
Romaine	Spinach
Watercress	Zucchini

*400 milligrams or more of sodium per serving.

Starchy vegetables such as corn, peas and potatoes are found on the bread/starch exchange list.

FRUIT LIST

Each item on the fruit list contains 15 grams of carbohydrates and 60 calories. Fruits are a wonderful addition to your food plan because of their complex carbohydrates, dietary fiber and other food components linked to good health. Also, they are readily available, taste good and are quick and easy to prepare.

Helpful Information About Fruit Exchanges

- Most fruits have about 2 grams of fiber per serving. Fruits that have 3 grams or more of fiber are marked with an asterisk (*).
- Fruits contain many important vitamins such as vitamin C.
- Fruits can be substituted for sugary desserts (fruit smoothie, fruit salad, a baked apple, etc.).

	Carbohydrates (in grams)	Protein (in grams)	Fat (in grams)	Calories
Fruit	15	—	—	60

FRUIT

Fresh, Frozen and Unsweetened Canned Fruit. Unless otherwise noted,
the serving sizes for one fruit serving are: ½ cup fresh or fruit juice or ¼ cup of dried

*Apple (2″ across, w/skin)	1 apple, 4 ounces
Applesauce (unsweetened)	½ cup
Apricots (medium, raw)	4 apricots
Apricots (canned)	½ cup, 4 halves or 4 ounces
Banana (9″ long)	½ banana or 3 ounces
*Blackberries (raw)	¾ cup
*Blueberries (raw)	¾ cup
Boysenberries	¾ cup
Cantaloupe (5″)	⅓ melon or 7 ounces
Cantaloupe cubes	1 cup
Caranbola (starfruit)	3 caranbola or 7½ ounces
Cherries (large, raw)	12 cherries or 3½ ounces
Cherries (canned)	½ cup
Crab apples	¾ cup or 2¾ ounces
Dewberries	¾ cup or 3 ounces
*Figs (2″, raw)	2 figs
Fruit cocktail (canned)	½ cup
Gooseberries	1 cup or 5 ounces
Grapefruit (medium)	½ grapefruit
Grapefruit (segments)	¾ cup
Grapes (small)	17 small
Honeydew melon (medium)	⅛ melon
Honeydew melon cubes	1 cup
Kiwi (large)	1 kiwi or 3¼ ounces
Mandarin oranges	¾ cup
Mango (small)	½ mango or 3 ounces
Mulberries	1 cup or 5 ounces
*Nectarine (1½)	1 nectarine or 5 ounces
Orange (2½)	1 orange or 6½ ounces
Papaya	1 cup or 8 ounces
Passion fruit	4 passion fruit or 4 ounces
Peach (2¾)	1 peach or ¾ cup
Peaches (canned)	½ cup or 2 halves
Pear (canned)	½ cup or 2 halves
*Pear w/skin	½ large or 1 small
Persimmon (medium)	2 persimmons
Pineapple (raw)	¾ cup

FRUIT (continued)

Plums	2 small or 5 ounces
*Pomegranate, raw	½ medium
*Raspberries	1 cup
Rhubarb (diced)	2 cups
*Strawberries (frozen)	1 cup
*Strawberries (raw)	1 ¼ cups
Tangelos	1 medium
Tangerines	2 small, 8 ounces
Watermelon	1 slice or 13 ½ ounces
Watermelon cubes	1 ¼ cups

DRIED FRUIT

*Apples	4 rings or ¾ ounce
*Apricots	7 halves or ¾ ounce
Dates	2 ½ medium
*Figs	1 ½
Prunes	3 medium or 1 ounce
Raisins	2 tbsp. or ¼ ounce

FRUIT JUICE

Apple juice/cider, grapefruit, orange, pineapple juices and most nectars	½ cup
Cranberry, grape and prune juices	⅓ cup
Lemon or lime juices	1 cup
Orange juice concentrate	2 tablespoons or 1 ounce

*3 grams or more of fiber per serving.

MEAT LIST

Each item on the meat exchange list contains approximately 7 grams of protein, some fat and no carbohydrates. The meat exchange is divided into three groups according to how much fat it contains.

Helpful Information About Meat Exchanges

- Most exchanges are based on 1-ounce servings of cooked meat.
- Broil, bake or grill without adding fats when preparing meats. Remove all visible fat.
- Add 1 extra fat exchange per ounce to any fried meat.
- Leave skin on poultry when roasting, but remove it before eating.

	Carbohydrates (in grams)	Protein (in grams)	Fat (in grams)	Calories
Meat				
Lean	—	7	3	55
Medium Fat	—	7	5	75
High Fat	—	7	8	100

LEAN MEAT AND SUBSTITUTES (FEWER THAN 3 GRAMS OF FAT)
Count as 1 meat exchange

Beef	Top round, boneless sirloin, flank steak, arm pot roast, sirloin tip roast, tenderloin, lean ground beef, London broil, strip steak, breakfast steak, filet mignon	1 ounce
Pork	Lean pork, such as fresh ham; canned cured, or boiled ham; *Canadian bacon; *tenderloin	1 ounce
Veal	All cuts are lean except for veal cutlets (ground or cubed)	1 ounce
Poultry	Chicken, turkey, Cornish hen (without skin)	1 ounce
Fish	Catfish, haddock, halibut, herring, orange roughy, trout salmon (not canned), sole or * tuna in water ($\frac{1}{4}$ cup)	1 ounce
Shellfish	*Clams, crab, lobster, scallops and shrimp	2 ounces
Game	Venison, rabbit	1 ounce
Cheese	Any cottage cheese	$\frac{1}{4}$ cup
	Grated parmesan	2t ablespoon
	*Fat-free cheese	1 ounce
	*Fat-free cream cheese	2 ounce
Other	Fat-free luncheon meat	1 ounce
	Egg whites	3
	Egg substitutes	$\frac{1}{4}$ cup
	Frankfurter (up to 3 grams fat/ounce)	1 ounce

ALTERNATIVE EXCHANGE

Beans, peas, lentils	1 cup = 2 bread + 1 meat

MEDIUM-FAT MEAT AND SUBSTITUTES (FEWER THAN 5 GRAMS OF FAT)
Count as 1 meat + $\frac{1}{2}$ fat

Beef	Ground beef, roast (rib, chuck, rump) and steak (cubed, Porterhouse, T-bone)	1 ounce
Pork	Chops, loin roast, Boston butts and cutlets	1 ounce

Lamb	Chops, leg and roast	1 ounce
Veal	Cutlet (ground or cubed, not breaded)	1 ounce
Poultry	Chicken (with skin), domestic duck or goose (with fat well drained) and ground turkey	1 ounce
	Turkey bacon	2 slices
Fish	*Tuna (canned in oil, drained),*canned salmon	¼ cup
Cheese	Light, skim or part-skim milk cheeses (i.e. mozzarella)	1 ounce
	Ricotta	¼ cup
Other	*Luncheon meat	1 ounce
	Egg	1
	Tofu	4 ounces
	Frankfurter (up to 5 grams fat/ounce)	1 ounce
	Liver, heart, kidney, sweetbreads (high in cholesterol)	1 ounce

THE FOLLOWING ARE HIGH IN FAT AND SHOULD BE USED SPARINGLY.
HIGH-FAT MEAT AND SUBSTITUTES (FEWER THAN 8 GRAMS OF FAT)
Count as 1 meat + 1 fat

Beef	USDA Prime cuts of beef such as ribs, brisket and *corned beef	1 ounce
Pork	Spareribs, ground pork, *pork sausage (patty or link)	1 ounce
Lamb	Patties (ground lamb)	
Cheese	All regular cheeses, such as American, Blue, Cheddar, Colby, Monterey Jack, Swiss	1 ounce
Other	*Luncheon meats, such as bologna, salami, pimento loaf	1 ounce
	* Sausage, Knockwurst, *Bratwurst	1 ounce
	Frankfurter (up to 8 grams of fat/ounce)	1 ounce
	Peanut butter (unsaturated fat)	1 tablespoon

*400 milligrams or more of sodium per serving.

MILK LIST

Each item on the milk exchange list contains 12 grams of carbohydrates, 8 grams of protein and 90 calories. Fat content and calories vary depending on the product you use. As a general rule, milk exchanges can be divided into four main categories (see below.)

Milk exchanges are the body's main source of calcium, the mineral needed for growth and repair of bones. It is important to consume at least 2 exchanges of milk daily.

Helpful Information About Milk Exchanges

- Many tasty dishes, including smoothies and sugar-free pudding, can be made with milk. Try the many different recipes in your cookbook.
- If you are used to whole milk products, you may find it easier to make the change slowly to lower fat foods. Try 2% fat milk first. When you're used to that, move to 1% fat milk. Your transition will be much easier if you decide later to change to fat-free milk.
- Grams of sugar appearing on the labels of sugar-free dairy products is not added sugar and should be ignored.
- Any dairy yogurt containing 100 calories or less per serving is one milk exchange.
- Frozen yogurt is found on the bread/starch exchange list.

Are you lactose intolerant?

- Drink milk in smaller amounts (i.e., ½ cup or less at a time).
- Use yogurt that contains live and active cultures instead of regular milk.
- Drink lactose-reduced milk.
- Add lactase drops to milk or use lactase pills.

	Carbohydrates (in grams)	Protein (in grams)	Fat (in grams)	Calories
Milk				
Fat-Free	12	8	trace	90
Very Low Fat	12	8	3	105
Low Fat	12	8	5	120
Whole	12	8	8	150

FAT-FREE MILK PRODUCTS
One Exchange = 1 Milk

Fat-free milk or ½ % milk	1 cup
Fat-free buttermilk	1 cup
Evaporated skim milk	½ cup
Dry nonfat milk	¼ cup
Dairy yogurt (fat free, sugar free)	8 ounces
Lactaid	1 cup

VERY LOW-FAT MILK PRODUCTS
One Exchange = 1 milk + ½ fat

1% milk	1 cup

LOW-FAT MILK PRODUCTS
One Exchange = 1 milk + 1 fat

1½ % milk or 2% milk	1 cup
Plain yogurt (low fat, sugar free)	8 ounces

WHOLE MILK (try to limit choices)
One Exchange = 1 milk + 2 fat

Whole Milk	1 cup
Evaporated whole milk	½ cup
Plain, whole, sugar-free yogurt	8 ounces

MISCELLANEOUS

Hot chocolate (sugar free)	1 packet = ½ milk
Pudding (sugar free, prepared with fat-free milk)	½ cup = ½ milk, ½ bread
Dairy shake (sugar free)	1 packet = 1 milk

CHEESE, OPTIONAL MILK EXCHANGE

Cheese	2 ounces
Cottage cheese	½ cup

*Choose cheese high in calcium and other nutriuents you expect to get from a milk exchange. Fat grams will count as fat exchange.

FAT

Each item on the fat exchange list contains 5 grams of fat and 45 calories. The Live-It plan limits your fat intake to 25 percent of your daily calorie total. One-half of your fat allotment comes from your lean meat choices. The other half is chosen from the fat exchange list.

Helpful Information About Fat Exchanges

- Saturated fat is found in meat and dairy products. Choose polyunsaturated and monounsaturated fats when possible for this exchange.
- Check labels carefully to find hidden fat.
- Use less added fat and spray-on vegetable coatings instead of oils to fry or cook foods.
- Add flavor to low-fat foods by using spices and marinating with non-fat dressings.

	Carbohydrates (in grams)	Protein (in grams)	Fat (in grams)	Calories
Fat	—	—	5	45

UNSATURATED FATS

Almond butter	1 teaspoon
Avocado	$\frac{1}{8}$ medium
Hot chocolate (sugar free)	1 packet = $\frac{1}{2}$ milk
Margarine	1 teaspoon
Margarine (light)	1 tablespoon
Mayonnaise	1 teaspoon
Mayonnaise (light)	1 tablespoon
Peanut butter	1 teaspoon
Nuts and seeds:	
Almonds (dry roasted)	6 whole
Cashews (dry roasted)	1 tablespoon
Chopped nuts	1 tablespoon
Peanuts	10 nuts or $\frac{1}{3}$ ounce
Pecans	20 small or 10 large
Pumpkin seeds	2 teaspoons

UNSATURATED FATS (CONTINUED)	
Walnuts	2 whole
Seeds, pinenuts, sunflower (without shells)	1 tablespoon
Oil (corn, cottonseed, safflower, soybean, sunflower, olive, peanut)	1 teaspoon
Olives	10 small or 5 large
*Salad Dressing	1 teaspoon
*Salad Dressing (lite)	1 tablespoon

SATURATED FATS (not recommended!)	
Bacon (cooked)	1 slice
Bacon grease	1 teaspoon
Butter	1 teaspoon
Butter (reduced fat)	1 tablespoon
Cheese spread	1 tablespoon
Chicken fat	1 teaspoon
Chitterlings	½ ounce
Chocolate (unsweetened)	1 ounce = 1 bread + 2 fats
Coconut (shredded)	2 tablespoons
*Coffee whitener (liquid)	2 tablespoons
*Coffee whitener (powder)	4 teaspoons
Cream cheese	1 tablespoon
Cream cheese (light)	2 tablespoons
Cream (half-and-half)	2 tablespoons
Sour cream	2 tablespoons
Sour cream (light)	3 tablespoons
Gravy	¼ cup
*Gravy (packaged)	½ cup
Lard	1 teaspoon
Meat fat	1 teaspoon
Salt pork	¼ ounce
Shortening	1 teaspoon
Whipping cream	1 tablespoon
*Whipped topping	3 tablespoons

*Read label: 5 grams fat = 1 fat exchange

FREE FOODS

The items on the free foods exchange list are foods very low in nutritional value and usually low in calories. Limit the total number of calories from this exchange to 50 per day.

Helpful Information About Free Foods

- Many of the foods or drinks listed contain sugar substitutes.
  First Place recommends using these in moderation only.

- Use these free foods to add the gourmet touches that make your meals as pleasant and attractive to serve as they are to eat.
- Check each label for serving size and caloric value.
- Measure free foods carefully. Calories add up fast!
- Free foods are not listed on your Commitment Record.

FREE FOODS

DRINKS

DRINKS	SNACKS
Bouillon or broth without fat	Candies (sugar free)
Carbonated drinks (sugar free)	Chewing gum (sugar free)
Carbonated water	Frozen novelty bar (sugar free)
Club soda	Gelatin (sugar free)
Coffee/tea	Pickles (unsweetened)
Drink mixes (sugar free)	
Iced Tea (sugar free)	
Tonic Water	

CONDIMENTS

Bacon bits (imitation)	Picante sauce
Barbecue sauce	Pickle relish
Butter flavoring (powdered)	Salad dressings (fat free)
Catsup	Salsa
Chili sauce	Sour cream (fat free)
Cocktail sauce	Soy sauce
Cocoa powder (unsweetened)	Steak sauce
Chocolate milk mix (sugar free)	Sugar substitutes
Coffee whiteners (nondairy)	Syrup (sugar free)
Cooking spray	Tabasco sauce
Enchilada sauce	Taco sauce
Fruit spreads (sugar free)	Teriyaki sauce
Horseradish	Tomato Sauce
Lemon or lime juice	Vinegar
Mayonnaise (fat free)	Whipped topping (fat free)
Mustard	Worcestershire sauce
Salt (seasoned)	

VEGETARIAN WAY

Most experts now agree that a well-planned vegetarian eating plan can supply all the nutrients your body needs for good health. In fact, research shows that eating the vegetarian way can reduce the risk for many health problems, such as coronary heart disease, high blood pressure, diabetes and some forms of cancer. Of course, any eating plan that's well balanced and includes a variety of foods can lower your risk for disease and improve your overall health and quality of life. While verses like the ones below clearly reveal that eating meat is appropriate, a vegetarian lifestyle can also be a healthy choice when well planned.

Healthy Vegetarian Eating

- A properly planned vegetarian diet includes adequate amounts of protein, calories, vitamins and minerals, and is low in saturated fat, total fat and cholesterol.
- Eat a variety of foods, including whole grains, vegetables, fruits, legumes, nuts, seeds and low-fat dairy products and eggs, if desired. Limit eggs to three yolks per week.
- Limit fats, oils and sweets.
- If you desire, eat up to three servings of milk, yogurt and cheese daily. Choose low-fat or nonfat varieties of these foods.
- Eat two to three servings daily of legumes, nuts, seeds, peanut butter, eggs and tofu. The following foods and servings count as your meat exchange:
    - 1 cup soy milk (choose products fortified with calcium, vitamin D and vitamin B_{12})
    - 1 cup cooked dry or canned beans or peas
    - 1 egg or 3 egg whites (limit three egg yolks per week)
    - 2 tablespoons nuts or seeds
    - ¼ to ½ cup tofu, soy cheese or tempeh
    - 1 tablespoon peanut or other nut butters
    - Eat four or more servings of vegetables daily.
    - Eat three or more servings of fruit daily.
    - Eat six or more servings of the bread/starch exchange daily.

Following the above plan should ensure that you get adequate amounts of protein, calories, iron, calcium, vitamin B_{12}, vitamin D and zinc, particularly if you eat dairy products and eggs. It's important to know, however, that eating vegetarian doesn't necessarily mean eating low fat. Many meat alternatives such as dairy can be higher in fat and calories than meat.

It may be necessary to combine specific foods during a vegetarian meal to obtain a complete protein. Animal proteins are considered complete proteins because they supply all the essential amino acids your body needs, while many plant-based proteins come up short in one or two.

Helpful Tips

- Use meat alternatives such as legumes or tofu in casseroles, stir-fry, chili and other meat dishes.
- Try substituting tofu, soy cheese or soy or rice milk for dairy products like milk, cheese and yogurt. Use only products that are calcium fortified.
- Add rice, pasta, barley, tabouli and other grains to soups, stew, chili and other dishes.
- Choose vitamin-fortified breakfast cereals.
- Enjoy a variety of fresh, frozen, canned and dried fruits and vegetables every day.
- Add extra vegetables to pasta dishes, soups, salads and casseroles.
- Add beans, peas, other legumes, nuts and seeds to salads to boost the protein content.
- Choose restaurants that offer a variety of vegetarian dishes. Ethnic restaurants, such as Asian and Indian, offer a variety of tasty vegetarian dishes.
- Many meat alternatives, such as cheese and nuts, are very high in fat and calories.
- Order salads, soups, breads and fruits if a restaurant doesn't offer vegetarian dishes.
- When traveling, call the airline at least 48 hours in advance to ask for a vegetarian meal.

RECOMMENDED RECIPE BOOKS

If you feel a bit overwhelmed at the thought of getting started with healthy eating, have no fear! Below is a list of recipe books that we think you will find most helpful as you begin your First Place journey.

Product # 2001	*First Place Favorites*
Published by:	LifeWay Press
Order:	1-800-4-GOSPEL

Product # 2002	*First Place Recipes*
Published by:	Oxmoor House
Order:	1-800-4-GOSPEL

ISBN # 1-58040-014-0	*Month of Meals #1 – Classic Cooking*
ISBN # 1-58040-015-9	*Month of Meals #2 – Ethnic Delights*
ISBN # 1-58040-016-7	*Month of Meals #3 – Meals in Minutes*
ISBN # 1-58040-017-5	*Month of Meals #4 – Old Time Favorites*
ISBN # 0-945448-34-1	*Month of Meals #5 – Vegetarian*

ISBN # 0-945448-76-7	*Brand-Name Diabetic Meals In Minutes*

ISBN # 0-945448-69-4	*Southern Style Diabetic Cooking*

Published by:	American Diabetes Association
Order:	1-800-232-6733

ISBN # 0-9654857-0-6	*Healthy Home Cooking*
Published by:	Healthy Home Cooking
Order:	7075 Red Fox Lane
	Cumming, GA 30040

ISBN # 0-89821-153-0	*Down-Home Diabetic Cookbook*
Published by:	Reiman Publications
Order:	1-800-558-1013

ISBN # 0-312-04330-9	*I Can't Believe This Has No Sugar Cookbook*
Published By:	St. Martin's Press
Order:	175 Fifth Ave., New York, NY 10010

COMMITMENT RECORD INFORMATION

The purpose of the Commitment Record (CR) is to aid you in keeping track of your accomplishments.

Begin a new CR on the morning of the day your class meets. This ensures that your CR is complete before your next meeting. Turn in the CR weekly to your leader.

DAY 1: Date _____

Morning _____

Midday _____

Evening _____

Snacks _____

_____ Meat _____
_____ Bread _____
_____ Vegetable _____
_____ Fruit _____
_____ Milk _____
_____ Fat _____

☐ Prayer
☐ Bible Study
☐ Scripture Reading
☐ Memory Verse
☐ Encouragement
Water _____

Exercise:
Aerobic _____

Strength _____
Flexibility _____

DAY 2: Date _____

Morning _____

Midday _____

Evening _____

Snacks _____

_____ Meat _____
_____ Bread _____
_____ Vegetable _____
_____ Fruit _____
_____ Milk _____
_____ Fat _____

☐ Prayer
☐ Bible Study
☐ Scripture Reading
☐ Memory Verse
☐ Encouragement
Water _____

Exercise:
Aerobic _____

Strength _____
Flexibility _____

DAY 3: Date _____

Morning _____

Midday _____

Evening _____

Snacks _____

_____ Meat _____
_____ Bread _____
_____ Vegetable _____
_____ Fruit _____
_____ Milk _____
_____ Fat _____

☐ Prayer
☐ Bible Study
☐ Scripture Reading
☐ Memory Verse
☐ Encouragement
Water _____

Exercise:
Aerobic _____

Strength _____
Flexibility _____

DAY 4: Date _____

Morning _____

Midday _____

Evening _____

Snacks _____

_____ Meat _____
_____ Bread _____
_____ Vegetable _____
_____ Fruit _____
_____ Milk _____
_____ Fat _____

☐ Prayer
☐ Bible Study
☐ Scripture Reading
☐ Memory Verse
☐ Encouragement
Water _____

Exercise:
Aerobic _____

Strength _____
Flexibility _____

FIRST PLACE CR

Name _____

Date _____ through _____

Week # _____ Calorie Level _____

Daily Exchange Plan

Level	Meat	Bread	Veggie	Fruit	Milk	Fat
1200	4-5	5-6	3	2-3	2-3	3-4
1400	5-6	6-7	3-4	3-4	2-3	3-4
1500	5-6	7-8	3-4	3-4	2-3	3-4
1600	6-7	8-9	3-4	3-4	2-3	3-4
1800	6-7	10-11	3-4	3-4	2-3	4-5
2000	6-7	11-12	4-5	4-5	2-3	4-5
2200	7-8	12-13	4-5	4-5	2-3	6-7
2400	8-9	13-14	4-5	4-5	2-3	7-8
2600	9-10	14-15	5	5	2-3	7-8
2800	9-10	15-16	5	5	2-3	9

You may always choose the high range of vegetables and fruits. Limit your high range selections to only one of the following: meat, bread, milk or fat.

_____ Loss   _____ Gain   _____ Maintain

_____ Attendance   _____ Bible Study
_____ Prayer   _____ Scripture Reading
_____ Memory Verse   _____ CR
_____ Encouragement:
_____ Exercise:
Aerobic _____

Strength _____
Flexibility _____

DAY 1: Date _____

Morning _____

Midday _____

Evening _____

Snacks _____

_____ Meat
_____ Bread
_____ Vegetable
_____ Fruit
_____ Milk
_____ Fat

☐ Prayer
☐ Bible Study
☐ Scripture Reading
☐ Memory Verse
☐ Encouragement
☐ Water

Exercise:
Aerobic _____

Strength _____
Flexibility _____

DAY 6: Date _____

Morning _____

Midday _____

Evening _____

Snacks _____

_____ Meat
_____ Bread
_____ Vegetable
_____ Fruit
_____ Milk
_____ Fat

☐ Prayer
☐ Bible Study
☐ Scripture Reading
☐ Memory Verse
☐ Encouragement
☐ Water

Exercise:
Aerobic _____

Strength _____
Flexibility _____

DAY 7: Date _____

Morning _____

Midday _____

Evening _____

Snacks _____

_____ Meat
_____ Bread
_____ Vegetable
_____ Fruit
_____ Milk
_____ Fat

☐ Prayer
☐ Bible Study
☐ Scripture Reading
☐ Memory Verse
☐ Encouragement
☐ Water

Exercise:
Aerobic _____

Strength _____
Flexibility _____

EXERCISE BASICS AND EXERCISE LOG

Many people who want to lose weight balk when then hear the word "exercise." Of course, it is possible lose weight without exercising; but when exercise is added to a nutritional eating plan, most of the weight loss will be from fat.[1]

BENEFITS OF EXERCISE

No one denies the fact that exercise is a great way to burn calories and lose weight. According to Dr. Couey, exercise makes several important contributions to any weight-control program.

> Exercise alters body composition in a desirable direction, thereby altering metabolism and making daily energy expenditures slightly high, even during rest. It also spends energy directly. Exercise also promotes the psychological benefits of looking and feeling healthy, and it reduces stress and stress-induced eating. Increased self-esteem accompanies these benefits, and this tends to support a person's resolve to persist in a weight-control effort.

Exercise has two other beneficial effects. First, the conditioned body is trained to use fatty acids, rather than glucose, as fuel. This means that after you have become conditioned, you will tend to burn more body fat during exercise than you did when you were out of condition. The best exercise for burning fat is not severely strenuous, but easy-paced to moderate exercise of long duration (30 minutes or more). Second, regular vigorous exercise will speed the metabolism slightly from a few hours, to up to 24 hours. The basal metabolism is stimulated by about 5% for as long as a day.[2]

As you consider the benefits of exercise, remember that if exercise is going to be helpful to your weight-loss endeavors, it must be active. So massages and machines don't count! The more muscles you move, the more kcalories[3] you spend. Also keep in mind that the number of kcalories you spend in any given activity depends more upon your weight than the pace of your exercise. For example, a person weighing 125 pounds who runs a six-minute mile burns off 90 kcalories; a person weighing 200 pounds, running the same six-minute mile, spends 140 kcalories. So you don't have to work fast to use up energy effectively.[4]

LIVE IT! AN EXERCISE LOG

Introduction

My walking program began in October 1984. After a few months of walking, I progressed to a walk-jog program and eventually began running. I ran for 15 years until I fell and tore the cartilage in my knee. After surgery to repair my knee, I am back to walking again. The use of a log to record my progress has not only encouraged and inspired me but has also served as a record of steady progress toward my own personal fitness goals.

We have included a sample exercise log for your convenience but encourage you to come up with a log that works well for you. Perhaps your log could be an extra page in your planner or a notebook you carry with you. You might also find it helpful to include a new Scripture passage on each weekly chart. Remember that His Word is filled with promises from the Bible just for you. Let God's Word bless you as your temple becomes fit.

The Guidelines for Cardiovascular-Respiratory Training and the 12-week charts for various aerobic exercises are used by permission of Dr. Dick Couey, author of *Happiness Is Being a Physically Fit Christian*. If you will follow Dr. Couey's guidelines, you should be able to obtain the proper CVR level in a 12-week period.

Guidelines for Cardiovascular-Respiratory (CVR) Training

Probably the worst thing you can do to begin your CVR program is grab your old tennis shoes, head for the nearest track and run at top speed. That could cause more harm than good. You must prepare yourself physically before you rush into cardiovascular exercise, or someone may have to rush you to the hospital. Please follow these guidelines and protect yourself from harm and injury.

1. *Get a medical examination, especially if you are over 35 years of age.* The medical examination should consist of a standard and stress electrocardiogram (ECG); resting and exercise blood pressure measurements; fasting blood sugar (glucose), cholesterol, triglyceride and high-density lipoprotein determinations; and evaluation of any orthopedic problem.

2. *Warm up before exercising.* Before beginning a CVR-training program, subject your total body to a proper warm-up. The warm-up is a precaution against unnecessary injuries and muscle soreness. It stimulates the heart and lungs moderately and progressively, as well as increases the blood flow and the blood and muscle temperatures gradually. It also prepares you mentally for the approaching strenuous workout.

   The following five-minute warm-up routine is recommended. During the first two minutes, do stretching exercises for arms, legs and back. During the third and fourth minutes, do sit-ups, push-ups and back raisers. During the final minute, walk or jog very slowly. Strive to walk or jog flat-footed as much as possible during the warm-up. This gives the tendons and ligaments in the feet and ankles a chance to stretch gradually, helping to avoid possible irritation from sudden stress.

3. *Cool down after exercise.* A cooldown is a tapering-off period after completion of the main workout and is as important to the body as the warm-up. During the CVR exercise, the large muscles of the legs provide a boost to the circulating blood and help return it to the heart and lungs where the exchange of oxygen and carbon dioxide takes place. As the muscle relaxes after exertion, blood fills the veins. It is not allowed to flow backward because of the valves in the veins. During exercise the squeezing action of the leg muscles provides about half of the pumping action, while the heart provides the other half. Walking or slow jogging, as in the cooldown, allows the muscle pump to continue to work until the total volume of blood being pumped is decreased to where the heart can handle it without help from the muscles.

   Always reduce your exercise pace very slowly, never abruptly. Do not stop instantly or sit down after you finish vigorous exercise or the blood will pool in your legs and you can faint from lack of blood to the brain.

4. *Exercise within your tolerance.* Do not push yourself to the extent of becoming overly tired. This is not only dangerous to your health, but defeats the purpose of exercise. If your body does not feel strong when you first awake, then you may be over-training.

5. *Progress slowly.* In exercise, hurrying your fitness development does not work; it merely invites trouble, such as muscle and joint injuries. You do not have to be first in everything you do. Take your time in your development of fitness. Gradually work up to your exercise goals.

6. *Get adequate rest and nutrition.* Your body may suffer from chronic fatigue if nutrition and rest are inadequate. No matter how hard or long you train the CVR system, optimal

results will not be achieved if nutrition and rest are poor.

7. *Exercise regularly.* Consistency and regularity are necessary for strengthening the CVR system. Spasmodic exercise can be dangerous. Your body is similar to a busy warehouse which is constantly moving goods in and out. Your exercise benefits cannot be stored; you need to add benefits daily. For every one week you cease to exercise, it takes nearly two weeks to regain the previous fitness level. Just as food intake is used up almost daily, so are the benefits of exercise unless they are replenished with more exercise.

8. *Wear proper shoes.* A faulty pair of exercise shoes can erase your good intentions to exercise as well as cause foot, leg or hip injuries. Good shoes can eliminate many of the hazards associated with walking or jogging, such as blisters and stress to the feet, legs and hips. Canvas tennis shoes are not good for walking and jogging, because they are too heavy and usually give poor foot support to the ligaments and bones. The training type of shoe used by most long-distance runners is recommended for jogging. These have a leather or nylon upper; a good, cushioned, multilayered, spongelike sole; and a strong heel counter. Quality is the key here. Exercise participants should buy the best shoe they can afford. Anyone unsure about what shoes to purchase would be wise to consult with someone who does a lot of long-distance running.

9. *Exercise cautiously in hot weather.* Never exercise vigorously when a combined temperature and humidity reach 165 or above (that is, 85 degrees F. and 80 percent humidity). Exercising over this recommended rate increases susceptibility to heat stroke. Never allow your body temperature to elevate above 105 degrees F. The best method of cooling your body during exercise is through evaporation. If humidity is above 80 percent, the evaporative processes of the body do not function properly, because the humid atmosphere cannot accept any more moisture that would come from the body. The body temperature will quickly rise above the danger level. If you live

in a hot and humid climate, you may have to exercise early in the morning or late at night. Wear clothes that allow your body to cool itself by evaporation. Never wear a sweat suit or rubberized suit that promotes sweating. Do not try to lose weight by sweating it off. This is not only dangerous, but you will gain the weight back when you drink fluids.

10. *Dress appropriately in cold conditions.* Most people overdress when they exercise in cold temperatures. Dress to feel comfortably warm during the exercise period without profuse sweating. Usually, one or two layers of light clothing, a knit cap covering the head and ears and knit gloves are sufficient. In very cold weather, a ski mask can be worn to protect the face and warm the air as it goes into the lungs. Always run with the wind in the latter stages of your exercise. The chill factor is increased when you run into the wind. If you run against the wind after sweating has increased, the chilling effects of the wind will be magnified.

Regular systemic CVR exercise is an important key to a happy life, as it promotes physical, mental, psychological and social fitness. It provides an outlet for emotional tensions and promotes self-confidence, wholesome social activity and good sportsmanship. It enhances the sense of general well-being that provides the willpower to confront and master the difficult personal challenges faced each day. But remember to heed these safety precautions: start slowly, progress slowly and do not overdo.

Walking Program

The walking program is for beginners or for individuals who have been inactive for four weeks or longer. These individuals should start with a walking program to slowly develop the leg muscles, ligaments, and tendons to prevent painful stress injuries. Hastening development by running too early only delays training because of time lost due to injuries. Furthermore, if activity is too strenuous at the start, previous ligament or joint problems could be aggravated, further delaying development.

For older people and those with a low level of CVR condition, walking initially provides enough physical stress to increase CVR fitness. If you are in poor physical condition because of prior inactivity or obesity, heed the following suggestions:

Begin walking at a normal, easy, steady pace. Swing your arms rhythmically, take in a deep breath on every fifth breath and release the air as much as possible. Acquire good jogging shoes, making sure to land on your heel first at foot strike. After several weeks, or as you become accustomed to walking, increase your speed to the point of walking a mile in 15 minutes or less. If you cannot maintain a brisk pace, periodically slow up for several seconds, then return to your more intense pace. After you have reached an intensity level of 45 minutes (at a pace of 15 minutes a mile), and providing you have no joint injuries, you can begin a walk-jog-walk program.

By the end of the eighth week, you should be able to maintain a 15-minute mile pace.

Week	Walk (min.)	Times Per Week
1	15	4
2	15	5
3	18	5
4	20	5
5	23	5
6	25	5
7	28	5
8	30	5
9	33	5
10	35	5
11	40	5
12	45	5

Walk-Jog-Walk Program

The walk-jog-walk technique of training represents the simplest approach for starting an exercise program to develop CVR fitness. This program has proven successful with school children, college students, medium-age adults and even senior adults.

Jogging is defined by most exercise physiologists as running at a pace equivalent to an 8-to-12-minute mile. A brisk walk is defined as walking at a pace equivalent to a 12-to-15-minute mile.

To begin your walk-jog-walk program, walk briskly for 10 minutes. Then begin jogging at a pace comfortable to your level of fitness. (A comfortable pace is one in which you could carry on a short-sentence conversation as you jog without interruptions from rapid breathing.) Jog for five minutes; then cool down by walking at a slower pace for eight minutes.

Week	Walk (min.)	Jog (min.)	Walk (min.)	Times Per Week
1	10	5	8	4
2	10	5	8	5
3	10	6	8	5
4	10	7	8	5
5	10	8	8	5
6	8	10	8	5
7	8	12	8	5
8	8	14	8	5
9	8	16	8	5
10	6	18	8	5
11	5	20	8	5
12	5	20	8	5

Check your pulse rate, making sure you reach your target heart rate of 70 percent.

Running Program

The running program is designed for individuals who want to progress further than the walk-jog-walk program or for well-conditioned individuals. The running program is designed for individuals who can run between a five- and eight-minute mile pace. So do not begin this program if you have been inactive for three weeks or longer. Progress slowly and enjoy your conditioning.

Week	Walk (min.)	Run (min.)	Walk (min.)	Times Per Week
1	3	20	5	5
2	3	20	5	5
3	3	22	5	5
4	3	22	5	5
5	3	25	5	5
6	3	25	5	5
7	3	28	5	5
8	3	28	5	5
9	3	32	5	5
10	3	35	5	5
11	3	40	5	5
12	3	40	5	5

Your running intensity should elevate your heart rate to the 70 percent level or higher.

Bicycling Program

To achieve a training effect with a bicycle, you must cycle slightly over twice as fast as you run to produce the same exercise heart rate. For bicycling to provide a heart rate stimulus of 70 percent of the difference between the maximum and resting rate. Also, warm up by cycling slowly for three minutes before attempting the specified time. Cool down by cycling slowly for three minutes at the conclusion of exercise.

Week	Warm-up (min.)	Cycling Time (min.)	Cooldown (min.)	Times Per Week
1	3	15	3	5
2	3	15	3	5
3	3	18	3	5
4	3	20	3	5
5	3	23	3	5
6	3	25	3	5
7	3	28	3	5
8	3	30	3	5
9	3	33	3	5
10	3	35	3	5
11	3	38	3	5
12	3	40	3	5

Adjust the bicycle seat to the position in which your extended leg has a slight bend at the knee joint.

Swimming Program

Many exercise physiologists and medical authorities advocate swimming as an ideal CVR conditioner. In comparison to jogging, there is less susceptibility to injury to the leg joints. Also, the upper body muscles are worked harder for greater muscle development. Disadvantages are the accessibility of a pool and availability of an open lane that will enable you to swim unbothered.

Continuous swimming is most beneficial for improving CVR fitness. Develop your endurance to the point where you can swim the length of the pool nonstop for several minutes. You may want to use different strokes. Changing strokes systematically will strengthen all the muscles used for the different movements in the various strokes.

Check your pulse rate after a series of swims, making sure that it is at the 70 percent intensity level. Be sure to first warm up by walking back and forth across the shallow end of the pool for a minimum of three minutes. Cool down by walking in the same manner. For comparison, 100 yards of swimming equals approximately 400 yards of jogging. Therefore, jogging two miles is equivalent to about a half mile of swimming.

Week	Warm-up (min.)	Swim Time (min.)	Cooldown (min.)	Times Per Week
1	3	8	3	5
2	3	8	3	5
3	3	10	3	5
4	3	12	3	5
5	3	15	3	5
6	3	18	3	5
7	3	20	3	5
8	3	23	3	5
9	3	25	3	5
10	3	25	3	5
11	3	28	3	5
12	3	30	3	5

Wear swim goggles to protect your eyes from chemical irritants in the pool water.

KNOW YOUR TRAINING HEART RATE

To be in good cardiovascular health, an individual must move continuously at his or her training heart range for a minimum of 20-25 minutes 3 to 4 times a week.

To take your pulse, use your first two fingers (not your thumb). Press lightly on your radial artery, close to your thumb on the inside of your wrist, or on your carotid artery, straight down from the corner of your eye, just under your chin. Count the number of beats for 10 seconds. Multiply by 6 to obtain your beats per minute. Be sure you are within your training heart rate zone.

Age	Maximum Heart Rate (beats per min.)	Training Heart Rate (75% of Mhr)	Training Heart Range (70-85% of Mhr)
20	200	150	140-170
25	195	146	137-166
30	190	142	133-162
35	185	139	130-157
40	180	135	126-153
45	175	131	123-149
50	170	127	119-145
55	165	124	116-140
60	160	120	112-136
65	155	116	109-135

During workouts, take your pulse when you start breathing hard. If you are below your zone, work a bit harder. Take your pulse every 5 to 10 minutes. If you go over your training heart rate, your exercise becomes anaerobic. You are no longer burning fat—you are burning lean body mass.

SAMPLE EXERCISE LOG

But they that wait upon the LORD shall renew their strength; they shall mount up with wings as eagles; they shall run, and not be weary; and they shall walk, and not faint (Isa. 40:31, *KJV*).

Date	Exercise	Distance	Time	My Thoughts Today
Week's Total				
Week's Average				
Week# _____ Year-To-Date				

SAMPLE BIBLE STUDY

MEMORY VERSE

*But seek first his kingdom and his righteousness, and
all these things will be given to you as well.*

MATTHEW 6:33

When embarking upon a journey toward better health, we need to seek
God's help and claim His promises. In Matthew 22:37 we discover the
place God wants to hold in our lives—first place. What a challenge!
Loving God halfheartedly is not enough. He wants complete commitment, and through that commitment to Him your life will be forever
changed.

In this week's study, you'll have the opportunity to search your heart
and examine your life. Are there areas of your life you have failed to surrender to Christ? If Christ is not first place in your thoughts, plans and
actions, what is?

DAY 1: TIME FOR WHAT YOU SEEK FIRST

Matthew 6:33 puts the pattern for Christian living in a nutshell: Seek
first the kingdom of God. In your busy life you cannot do everything.

However, the thing you can decide is what to do first. What you choose first, over time, takes first place in your life.

If you look at the entries in your calendar or checkbook for the past month, you might be surprised by what has been first place in your life lately.

1. List areas to which you find yourself giving the most time and effort.

God knows that things other than spiritual priorities tend to become the focus of our lives. Your checkbook and calendar will remind you of this fact.

2. In Matthew 6:25 Jesus mentioned some of the things that divert our attention from His priorities in our lives. What are those things?

Jesus wasn't saying that what you eat, drink or wear is not important; He simply stressed that you need not worry about them. These concerns must never take first place in your life. Instead, Jesus has challenged you to learn some simple lessons about God's provision.

3. According to Matthew 6:26-30, what does God want you to learn from the birds and flowers?

When you see the lessons of His provision for the birds and flowers, you will begin to understand how God knows and meets your needs. Philippians 4:19 also reminds you of His promise. He didn't say He would meet some or a few of your needs, but *all* your needs.

4. Do you believe this promise applies to you? ❑ Yes ❑ No

5. What needs do you have in your life now that you can turn over to God?

As Christians, the desire to give Christ first place in every area of our lives must be foremost. *Saying* Christ is first and *living* with Christ in first place are different matters. When Christ comes first, your life will change. You will make decisions based on new commitments. You will schedule time based on new priorities.

Use this week's memory verse to keep this commitment in focus. Listen to the CD while exercising. Display the card in the bathroom and/or kitchen and read it each time you are in that room. Memorizing Scripture will reinforce your commitment to keep Christ in first place and direct your thoughts and actions toward Christ and His kingdom.

✝ *Thank You Lord, for the promise to meet my needs through Your Son, Jesus.*

Lord, help me to trust You and give You first place in my life this week.

DAY 6: REFLECTIONS

You've been studying the Bible for five days; this may be a new experience for you or it may already be a daily part of your life. In either case these studies will help you establish new patterns for your life. Bible study requires a greater priority on the spiritual level of your life than the physical elements of other commitments require.

The Reflection section at the end of each week will introduce a powerful spiritual resource—praying through the Scriptures. Whether this is your first or fifth Bible study for First Place, this section will help you overcome those things in your life that have become strongholds. If you are not familiar with praying through Scripture, this section will teach you how. For repeaters, this section will be a refresher and will reiterate those things you've learned.

Praying through Scripture is the process of taking a verse and praying it back to God in your own words. Beth Moore's book *Praying God's Word*[1] explains the process.

You can learn much about letting God be in control and overcoming your own strongholds through Beth Moore's own testimony.

I've been educated in the power of God and His Word through field trips of my own failure, weakness, and past bondage . . . I didn't discover what a vital part of my liberation this approach has been until long after I had begun practicing it. I suddenly realized it was no accident that I was finally set free from some areas of bondage that had long hindered the abundant, effective, Spirit-filled life in me.[2]

Beth tells us that a stronghold may be an addiction, an unforgiving spirit toward a person who has hurt you, or despair over loss; and it demands so much of your emotional and mental energy that your abundant life is strangled. You, too, can break down the spiritual strongholds in your life as you pray through the Scriptures.[3]

The process isn't complicated: You take a particular verse and pray that verse to the Lord, personalizing the words. The following are examples of praying Scripture. Ask the Lord to reveal the strongholds in your life as you pray each one.

✝ *Lord, help me overcome the strongholds in my life. I long for You to be first. I want to seek first Your kingdom and Your righteousness. Thank You for your promise to give me the other things I need (see Matthew 6:33).*

Father, when Your words come to me, help me to eat them; make them my joy and my heart's delight, for I bear Your name, O Lord God Almighty (see Jeremiah 15:16).

God, through the victories You give, may Christ's glory be great (see Psalm 21:5).

ENDNOTES

Introduction

1. Meginnis and Foege, "Actual Causes of Death in the United States," *Journal of American Medical Association,* 1993, quoted in John Graham, source unknown.
2. Jim Ritter, *Chicago Sun Times,* September 18, 1997.
3. Dr. Richard Couey, *Nutrition for God's Temple* (Nashville, TN: LifeWay Press, 1994), pp. 120, 121.

Chapter Two

1. Zig Ziglar, *See You at the Top* (New York: Pelican Publishing Company, 1975), n.p.
2. Oswald Chambers, *My Utmost for His Highest: An Updated Edition in Today's Language,* ed. James Reimann (Grand Rapids, MI: Discovery House Publishers, 1992), n.p.

Chapter Four

1. Ziglar, *See You at the Top,* p. 288.
2. Tim Hansel, *Holy Sweat* (Dallas, TX: Word Publishing, 1987), p. 117.
3. Ibid., p. 157.

Chapter Five

1. William Heston, "Putting the Past in Perspective," (paper presented at the First Place Conference, Woodmont, Georgia, October 1997), n.p.
2. Clyde Francis Lytle, ed., *Leaves of Gold: An Anthology of Prayers, Memorable Phrases, Inspirational Verse and Prose* (Fort Worth, TX: Brownlow Publishing Company, Inc., 1938), p. 108.

Chapter Seven

1. Couey, *Nutrition for God's Temple*, n.p.
2. Bill Hybels, *Honest to God* (Grand Rapids, MI: Zondervan Publishing, 1990), pp. 169-171.
3. Ibid.

Chapter Nine

1. Chambers, *My Utmost for His Highest*, n.p.

Appendix C

1. Couey, *Nutrition for God's Temple*, p. 122.
2. Ibid., pp. 122, 123.
3. The term "calorie" is in popular use, although this usage is not technically correct, since a calorie is only 1/1000 as large as a kilocalorie. A kilocalorie is defined as a measure of energy: the amount of heat needed to raise the temperature of 1 kilogram of water 1 degree Celsius.
4. Couey, *Nutrition for God's Temple*, p. 123.

Appendix D

1. Beth Moore, *Praying God's Word* (Nashville, TN: Broadman and Holman, 2000).
2. Ibid., p. 2.
3. Ibid., p. 3.

MINISTRY CONTACT PAGE

For more information about First Place, please contact:

First Place
7401 Katy Freeway
Houston, TX 77024
Phone: 1-800-72-PLACE (727-5223)
E-mail: info@firstplace.org
Website: www.firstplace.org

First Place was founded under the providence of God and with the conviction that there is a need for a program which will train the minds, develop the moral character and enrich the spiritual lives of all those who may come within the sphere of its influence.

First Place is dedicated to providing quality information for development of a physical, emotional and spiritual environment leading to a life that honors God in Jesus Christ. As a health-oriented program, First Place will stress the highest excellence and proficiency in instruction with a goal of developing within each participant mastery of all the basics of a lasting healthy lifestyle, so that all may achieve their highest potential in body, mind and spirit. The spiritual development of each participant shall be given high priority so that each may come to the knowledge of Jesus Christ and God's plan and purpose for each life.

First Place offers instruction, encouragement and support to help members experience a more abundant life. Please contact the First Place national office in Houston, Texas at (800) 727-5223 for information on the following resources:

❖ Training Opportunities

❖ Conferences/Rallies

❖ Workshops

❖ Fitness Weeks

Send personal testimonies to:

First Place

7401 Katy Freeway
Houston, TX 77024

Phone: **(800) 727-52223**
Website: ***www.firstplace.org***

THE BIBLE'S WAY TO WEIGHT LOSS

First Place—the Bible-Based Weight-Loss Program
Used Successfully by over 1/2 Million People!

Are you one of the millions of disheartened dieters who've tried one fad diet after another without success? If so, your search for a successful diet is over! First Place is the proven weight loss program born over 20 years ago in the First Baptist Church of Houston.

But First Place does much more than help you take off weight and keep it off. This Bible-based program will transform your life in every way—physically, mentally, spiritually and emotionally. Now's the time to join!

Group Starter Kit
ISBN 08307.28708

Every leader needs a First Place Group Starter Kit. This kit has everything group leaders need to help others change their lives forever by giving God first place! Kits include:

- *Leader's Guide*
- *Member's Guide*
- *Giving Christ First Place Bible Study* with Scripture Memory CD
- *Choosing to Change* by Carole Lewis
- *First Place* by Carole Lewis with Terry Whalin
- *Orientation* Video
- *Nine Commitments* Video
- *Food Exchange Plan* Video

Member Kit
ISBN 08307.28694

Each member needs a First Place Group Starter Kit. All the material is easy to understand and spells out principles members can easily apply in their daily lives. Kit includes:

- *Member's Guide*
- *Choosing to Change* by Carole Lewis
- 13 Commitment Records
- Four Motivational Audiocassettes
- *Prayer Journal*
- Scripture Memory Verses: *Walking in the Word*

ESSENTIAL FIRST PLACE PROGRAM MATERIALS

Giving Christ First Place Bible Study
with Scripture Memory CD
ISBN 08307.28643

Everyday Victory for Everyday People Bible Study
with Scripture Memory CD
ISBN 08307.28651

Available at your local Christian bookstore or by calling **1-800-4-GOSPEL**.

To see other First Place resources, visit **www.gospellight.com/firstplace**.

Inspiration &Information Every Month!

Subscribe Today!

Every newsletter gives you:

- **New recipes**
- **Helpful articles**
- **Food tips**
- **Inspiring testimonies**
- **Coming events**
- **And much more!**

Subscribe online at www.firstplace.org or return the coupon below.

Please enter my subscription to the First Place Newsletter.
Please print legibly. Allow 4-8 weeks for delivery of first issue.

Name_____

Address_____

City, State, Zip_____

Home Phone (____)_____

Work Phone (____)_____

Email Address_____

❏ My check for $12 is enclosed; $14.99 for subscription outside continental USA.
(Please make checks payable to First Place.)

❏ Charge to: (circle one)

      Visa   MasterCard   Discover   American Express

Card# _____-_____-_____-_____Expires_____

Signature_____

First Place Newsletter • 7401 Katy Freeway • Houston, Texas 77024
Phone: (800) 727-5223 • Fax: (713) 688-8098 • www.firstplace.org

042643

A Must-Have Publication for All First Place Leaders & Members!

www.gospellight.com/firstplace

Strengthen Your Faith!

Communication @ Work
H. Norman Wright
How to get along with anyone
in the workplace and at church

Paperback
ISBN 08307.27779

**Where Hearts Are Shared
Cookbook**
Jane Hansen
Simple recipes and tips for
entertaining from women
around the world

Hardcover
ISBN 08307.28937

**Moments Together for
Couples**
Dennis and Barbara Rainey
Daily devotions for drawing
near to God and one another

Hardcover
ISBN 08307.17544

Beauty Restored
Me Ra Koh
Finding life and hope after
date rape

Paperback
ISBN 08307.27612

Living the Spirit-Formed Life
Jack Hayford
Growing in the 10 principles of
Spirit-filled discipleship

Paperback
ISBN 08307.27671

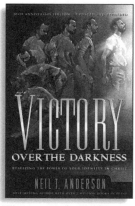

Victory over the Darkness
Neil T. Anderson
Realizing the power of your
identity in Christ

Paperback
ISBN 08307.25644

Great Reading for Your Spiritual and Physical Health!

Communication: Key to Your Marriage
H. Norman Wright
A practical guide to creating a happy, fulfilling relationship

Paperback
ISBN 08307.25334

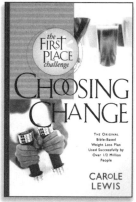

Choosing to Change
Carole Lewis
Inspiring introduction to the First Place weight-loss plan

Paperback
ISBN 08307.28627

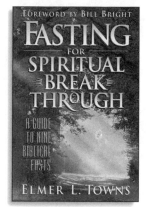

Fasting for Spiritual Breakthrough
Elmer L. Towns
Nine biblical fasts to strengthen your faith

Paperback
ISBN 08307.18397

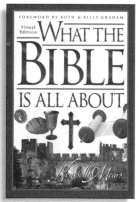

What the Bible Is All About Visual Edition
Henrietta Mears
Over 500 full-color photographs and illustrations

Hardcover
ISBN 08307.24311

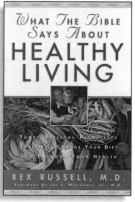

What the Bible Says About Healthy Living
Rex Russell, M.D.
Three biblical principles that will change your diet and improve your health

Paperback
ISBN 08307.18583

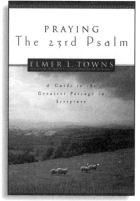

Praying the 23rd Psalm
Elmer L. Towns
Great devotional reading that will bring comfort and peace to believers

Paperback
ISBN 08307.27760

Regal
FROM GOSPEL LIGHT

Available at your local Christian bookstore. www.regalbooks.com